Aroun

Childcare s

June Statham a

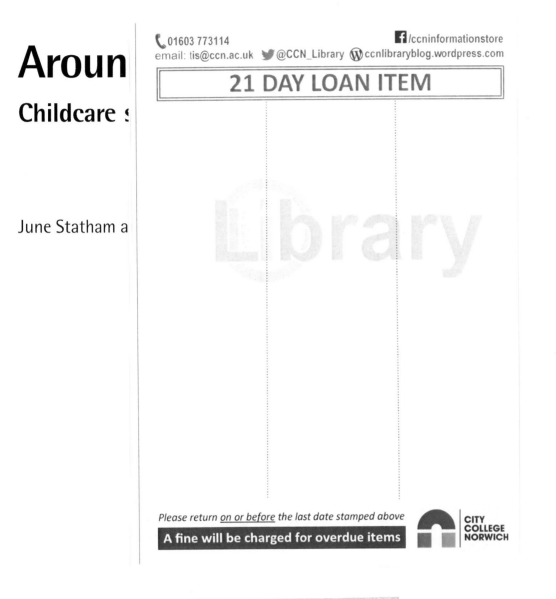

First published in Great Britain in June 2003 by

The Policy Press
Fourth Floor, Beacon House
Queen's Road
Bristol BS8 1QU
UK

Tel no +44 (0)117 331 4054
Fax no +44 (0)117 331 4093
E-mail tpp-info@bristol.ac.uk
www.policypress.org.uk

Reprinted 2004

British Library Cataloguing in Publication Data
A catalogue record for this book is available from the British Library.

Library of Congress Cataloging-in-Publication Data
A catalog record for this book has been requested.

Published for the Joseph Rowntree Foundation by The Policy Press

ISBN 1 86134 502 X

June Statham and **Ann Mooney** are Senior Research Officers at the Thomas Coram Research Unit, Institute of Education, University of London.

The **Joseph Rowntree Foundation** has supported this project as part of its programme of research and innovative development projects, which it hopes will be of value to policy makers, practitioners and service users. The facts presented and views expressed in this report are, however, those of the authors and not necessarily those of the Foundation.

Cover design by Qube Design Associates, Bristol
Printed in Great Britain by Hobbs the Printers Ltd, Southampton

Contents

List of tables

Acknowledgements

We would like to thank all those who
participated in this project and kindly gave up
their time to talk to us or complete
questionnaires. Without their help this study
would not have been possible. We are also
grateful for the help given to us by OFSTED
(Office for Standards in Education). Our
Advisory Group – Susan Bowles (DfES,
Department for Education and Skills), Jane
Costello (DfES), Rebecca Gill (TUC, Trades Union
Congress), Christine Goode (OFSTED), Ivana La
Valle (NatCen, National Centre for Social
Research), Eva Lloyd (National Early Years
Network) and Megan Pacey (Daycare Trust) –
have provided valuable help and advice. We
would like to thank them and also Barbara
Ballard, our research manager, and Shirley Dex,
the programme adviser. We appreciate too the
administrative assistance provided by Annabelle
Stapleton at the Thomas Coram Research Unit.
Although the study has benefited greatly from
the contributions of all those mentioned above,
the authors remain responsible for the opinions
expressed in this report and for any errors it may
contain.

Introduction

With the growth in a service-based economy and 24-hour operation, more parents are likely to be working outside the traditional hours of 9 to 5. There has been a rapid expansion of childcare provision since the introduction of the National Childcare Strategy in 1998, with further expansion planned, yet we have little information about how childcare services may be meeting the needs of parents working at atypical times. This study was designed to look at the barriers to developing services to cover atypical working hours and what may facilitate service development.

The National Childcare Strategy

The National Childcare Strategy (DfEE, 1998), launched in England in May 1998, marked a significant shift in government policy away from the view that childcare is a private issue for parents and that finding and paying for childcare should be left to families rather than the state, unless a child is 'at risk'. Previous policy based on this view had resulted in a fragmented early childhood service and reliance on the private market to meet parents' childcare needs (Mooney and Munton, 1997). At the time the Labour government took power in 1997, there was what the Daycare Trust described as a "huge childcare gap" (Kelleher, 2000, p 1), with only one registered childcare place for every nine children under the age of eight. The aim of the National Childcare Strategy is to increase the availability of affordable, accessible and good quality childcare in every neighbourhood.

In the relatively short time since the strategy has been in effect, a major expansion of childcare and early years services has taken place.

Between March 1998 and March 2000, the number of day nurseries, out-of-school clubs and holiday schemes rose substantially, although the number of pre-school playgroups and childminders fell (DfEE, 2000). Further expansion is planned for the future. By 2006, the government aims to increase the number of childcare places for over 2 million children (Strategy Unit, 2002). Part-time nursery education is available to all four-year-olds and will be available to all three-year-olds by 2004. Local Sure Start programmes, which benefit children from birth to age three in disadvantaged areas, will be operating in over 500 areas and will also help to boost the number of childcare places (Strategy Unit, 2002).

The expansion of childcare and early years services is seen by the government as making a significant contribution to a number of the targets set out in the government's Public Service Agreements. These targets include: to increase employment over the economic cycle; to reduce the number of children in households with no one in work; and to increase the employment rates of people in disadvantaged areas and groups including lone parents. For example, the intention is to provide a childcare place in the most disadvantaged areas for every lone parent entering employment (DfEE, 2001). The government has set a target to achieve 70% labour market participation among lone parents by 2010 and to eradicate child poverty by 2020, and has stated that "childcare is essential for these objectives to be met" (Strategy Unit, 2002, p 10).

Growing demand for childcare

Although the declining birth rate means that the number of children in the population is falling, increasing maternal employment rates, changes in the patterns of work and an increase in the number of lone parents mean that demand for childcare will grow. Employment among women with young children has risen sharply since the latter half of the 1980s. The employment rate among women with a child under five doubled between 1984 and 2000, from 27% to 54%, and far exceeded the rate of increase among all women over this period (Brannen et al, 1997; Bell, 2000; Twomey, 2001). While part-time employment has continued to predominate among employed women with young children, the growth in full-time employment has recently outstripped part-time growth. There is therefore an increasing need for childcare services to cover both part-time and full-time working hours.

New working patterns

A characteristic of the labour market in the UK is the long hours culture (HM Treasury and DTI, 2003). Working hours have increased over the past 10 years for both men and women, and especially among managers and professionals. Full-time employees in the UK now work the longest hours in Europe. Despite the Working Time Directive[1] (European Union, 1998), one in six workers now puts in more than a 48-hour week, and around 11% of full-time employees work 60 or more hours a week, particularly fathers with dependent children (Hogarth et al, 2001; TUC, 2002).

Non-standard or atypical working hours is not a new phenomenon. Professions such as nursing and the police and some manufacturing industries have always required shift work, but atypical working is becoming more widespread. In fact, the term 'atypical' is probably a misnomer, since the growth of a '24-hour society' has meant that more people are now working outside the 'standard' 9 to 5 day, Monday to

Friday, than are working solely within it. In a survey of 7,500 employees, only 35% worked a standard week (defined as Monday to Friday, starting between 8am and 10am and finishing between 4pm and 6pm), while 15% worked on Sundays and one in eight worked both Saturday and Sunday (Hogarth et al, 2001). Increasing numbers of employers depend on round-the-clock availability of their workers, often at short notice or for unpredictable shift patterns (Daycare Trust, 2000).

Since much of the economy is dependent on new working patterns, many parents who want to work have no choice other than to work atypical hours. In a survey of parents' demand for childcare undertaken for the Department for Education and Skills, 33% of households (with a child aged 14 or under) had a parent who worked long hours (over 45 hours a week) and 16% had a parent who worked shifts (Woodland et al, 2002). Overall, around a third (35%) of parents had an atypical work pattern[2]. La Valle et al (2002), in a study of the impact of parental work at atypical times on family life, found a higher incidence. They used a broader definition of atypical work hours[3] and found that in most two-parent families, one or both parents frequently worked atypical hours, while just over a half of working lone mothers worked atypical hours.

There is considerable diversity in the circumstances of parents who work non-standard hours. People in professional and managerial positions may be compensated for working long or unsociable hours by high salaries. However, shift work and jobs that involve irregular hours are usually linked to low pay and job insecurity (Daycare Trust, 2000). A study of self-employed parents (Bell and La Valle, 2003) found that self-employed mothers fell into two distinct groups: those with employees, who were mostly in professional and managerial jobs and were particularly likely to work long hours and to use formal childcare services; and those without employees, who were most likely to be found in part-time manual jobs. Both groups of self-employed women were more likely than their employed counterparts to report unmet demand

---

[1] The EU Working Time Directive (1998) specifies a limit on working hours of 48 hours, although the UK allows opt-outs for those employees who agree and for some employers.

[2] Defined as shift-working, working irregular hours and/or days, or working at weekends.

[3] Defined as work at weekends and work during the week before 8.30am and after 5.30pm.

for childcare. However, whereas the difficulties for those with employees might be linked to the amount of childcare required and the need for provision at 'non-standard' times, for self-employed mothers without employees, these difficulties might be related to a lack of affordable childcare as many were in low paid jobs. Finding childcare that is both available *and* affordable for the hours needed may therefore be a particular problem. Solutions are needed which meet the needs and circumstances of all families, not just those that can afford to pay high childcare fees (Moss et al, 1998).

Childcare services

How has the childcare 'industry' responded to the growth in non-standard working hours? Information on the availability of childcare to cover such hours is limited. Nannies and childminders are two types of formal childcare that may meet the needs of parents working atypical hours, although the cost of employing a nanny is beyond the reach of the majority of parents. Childminders could be well placed to provide a flexible service, although the extent to which they do so is uncertain. In a survey of 250 childminders in both England and Wales (Moss et al, 1995), 85% said they were prepared to offer flexible hours to fit the needs of parents with irregular working hours. However, findings from two further studies suggest that most childminders want to restrict their childminding to conventional daytime hours (Callender, 2000; Mooney et al, 2001).

Little is known about the extent to which other forms of provision offer a service outside the typical working day. Whereas the majority of day nurseries and childminders provide at least seven hours of care a day, pre-school playgroups and out-of-school care provision usually last only three to four hours a day (Callender, 2000). An audit of childcare in Wales (Statham et al, 1996) noted the existence of nurseries set up by health authorities to provide childcare for hospital staff who worked irregular hours, but was unable to provide detailed information on this service. Facing a staffing crisis, the NHS has recognised the need to address childcare. Under the NHS childcare programme (NHS, 2000), a childcare coordinator has been appointed in every NHS Trust and an increase in childcare provision is anticipated, which is likely to extend beyond typical working hours.

A study by the Daycare Trust for the Department for Education and Skills, which aimed to identify the demand for and availability of childcare for parents working shifts and atypical hours, surveyed 40 Early Years Development and Childcare Partnerships (EYDCPs) in England. Fewer than half were able to identify any childcare services that could meet the needs of families working outside the hours of 8am to 6pm, although 86% knew of local employers who required employees to work at these atypical times. In addition to this survey, the study looked at examples of employers providing flexible work options and help with childcare, the demand for childcare at atypical hours and how it is met in other countries, and the views of parents working atypical hours about their childcare needs (DfES, 2001a).

Parents working atypical hours and childcare

Previous research has shown that parents who work at atypical times generally rely on partners/ ex-partners or informal providers such as grandparents to meet their childcare needs (DfES, 2001a; La Valle et al, 2002; Woodland et al, 2002; Skinner, 2003). In fact, both among two-parent and lone-parent working households, irrespective of hours worked, more families had used grandparents for childcare in the past year than other types of formal or informal provision (Woodland et al, 2002, table 3-8, p 33). This may reflect a preference for informal care, but lack of flexible, affordable services among other types of childcare provision may also be a factor (DfES, 2001a; La Valle et al, 2002).

In summary, a fair amount is known about parents' working hours and use of childcare, but much less about the extent to which childcare services are available during non-standard hours, and the particular issues from the providers' perspective in offering such provision.

Aims of the study

It was against the above background that the study was developed, with the aim of examining the factors that prevent or facilitate childcare providers offering a service that covers atypical working hours.

Methodology

The study adopted a multi-method approach and included a survey of all English Early Years Development and Childcare Partnerships (EYDCPs), surveys of national childcare organisations and childcare providers, and case studies of providers offering atypical hours childcare, defined as outside 8am to 6pm or at times that varied. We did not seek the views of parents about atypical hours and childcare services, as this has been addressed in recent studies referred to above (DfES, 2001a; La Valle et al, 2002).

A survey of EYDCPs

EYDCPs currently have responsibility in each local authority for implementing the National Childcare Strategy, although it has been announced that, in future, responsibility should be given to local authority chief executives, who will consult with local partners through EYDCPs or other appropriate means (Strategy Unit, 2002, p 47). The partnerships conduct regular childcare audits and draw up plans, which document the expansion of provision, unmet demand for places, childcare provider training and quality assurance. As such they have a good knowledge of childcare provision in their area and of what may be the barriers to meeting parents' needs for atypical hours childcare.

A questionnaire was sent to all 150 English EYDCPs in February 2002. After a reminder, using electronic mail, 114 questionnaires were returned representing 76% of all EYDCPs. The questionnaire elicited information on:

- the demand for childcare services offering atypical hours;
- how demand was being met;

- the need to develop services and the barriers and facilitators to development;
- examples of childcare providers meeting the needs of parents working atypical hours.

A survey of national childcare organisations

Telephone interviews were conducted with representatives from the following six national childcare organisations: Daycare Trust, Kids Clubs Network (KCN), National Association of Children's Information Services (NACIS), National Childminding Association (NCMA), National Day Nurseries Association (NDNA), and the Pre-School Learning Alliance (PLA). The interviews took 30 minutes on average and covered the organisation's views on childcare for atypical working hours, the demand for and extent of provision, factors that facilitate or hinder service development, and examples of good practice.

A survey of childcare providers

Using information from the survey of EYDCPs, two authorities were selected that indicated that they had a demand for atypical hours childcare that was 'partly' met. One was a small unitary authority in the south of England (Authority A) and the other a large metropolitan authority in the north of England (Authority B). A random sample of 300 formal childcare providers[4] in each of the two authorities was surveyed by a postal questionnaire: a total of 400 childminders, 70 day nurseries, 70 out-of-school services and 60 pre-school playgroups. Table 1.1 gives details of childcare provision in each authority, the proportion of each type of provider surveyed and response rates. There are a number of reasons why we sampled more childminders. From previous work (for example Mooney et al, 2001) we anticipated a lower response rate from childminders, although in practice we were able to achieve a similar response rate from all provider types (Table 1.1). Childminders also provide more childcare places overall than do day nurseries (DfES, 2001b), and are more likely to offer childcare at atypical times compared to

---

[4] Formal childcare services refer to childminders and group-based provision such as centres or day nurseries, pre-schools (that is, playgroups) and out-of-school clubs. Informal childcare, on the other hand, refers to care provided by relatives and friends.

institutions such as pre-school playgroups, which have traditionally not offered a service for working parents (see Chapter 2).

The questionnaire, which was piloted, collected information about services, willingness to provide childcare outside standard working hours (defined as 8am to 6pm), the barriers to providing such childcare and what, if anything, would act as an encouragement to do so. The Office for Standards in Education (OFSTED), which now has responsibility for the regulation of childcare services and holds the database of registered providers, undertook the random selection of providers and distributed the questionnaire on our behalf. After a reminder, 365 replies were received, a response rate of 61%. However, 10% of those responding were not currently offering a childcare service, so the analysis is based on the remaining 327 responses (Table 1.1).

Of those providers responding, most were well established. Around two thirds of the day nurseries and childminders and the majority of the pre-school playgroups had been running for five years or more, although fewer out-of-school services had been running this long. Out-of-school services provided childcare for

school-aged children, as would be expected, but so too did most childminders and a third of day nurseries.

Since our samples of day nurseries, out-of-school and pre-school playgroup providers are small, we have provided numbers rather than percentages for each separate type of provision. We avoided combining the results for these three group-based providers because each type of provision is very different, and to combine the results would be misleading. In drawing conclusions from this data we have also taken into account the findings from the survey of EYDCPs, the interviews with national childcare organisations and case studies.

Case studies

Based on information provided by the six national childcare organisations and the surveys of EYDCPs and childcare providers, we planned to identify six providers offering a service to meet the needs of employees working atypical hours. We wanted to include different types of provider and atypical hours childcare covering weekend and overnight as well as early morning and late evening hours. This proved more

Table 1.1: Details of responses in survey of childcare providers in each authority

		Childminders	Day nurseries	Out-of-school services	Pre-school playgroup	Total
Authority A	Number of providers[a]	464	71	85	69	689
	Number surveyed	200	35	35	30	300
	% of total registered	23	49	41	43	44
	Number responding	109	29	26	18	182
	Response rate (%)	55	83	74	60	61[b]
Authority B	Number of providers[a]	1,181	115	243	111	1,650
	Number surveyed	200	35	35	30	300
	% of total registered	17	30	14	27	18
	Number responding	112	13	14	6	145
	Response rate (%)	56	37	40	20	48[b]
Totals	Number of providers[a]	1,645	186	328	180	2,339
	Number sampled	400	70	70	60	600
	% of total sampled	24	38	21	33	26
	Number of providers[a]	221	42	40	24	327
	Response rate (%)	55	60	57	40	55[b]

[a] According to the database of registered providers held by OFSTED.

[b] This does not include those who were no longer offering a service, but returned the questionnaire.

difficult than anticipated, since, as we shall see in Chapter 2, none of the providers surveyed were currently providing late evening, weekend or overnight care.

A number of sources, including the Children's Information Service and the NHS Childcare Toolkits (Daycare Trust, 2001 and 2002), were therefore used to identify our case studies. It took some time and many telephone calls. A number of false trails were followed before we were successful in finding two childminder networks, a community nanny scheme, and two children's centres offering childcare outside standard working hours. Short case studies were constructed based on telephone interviews, which focused on how the service was set up, any difficulties faced and how these had been overcome, the response from parents and lessons for future practice.

Summary

Working atypical hours is now more common in the general population than only working the standard 9 to 5, Monday to Friday week. Many parents of young children will be working atypical hours, either by necessity or choice. Although the government's National Childcare Strategy has led to a major expansion in childcare and early years services since 1998, little is known about how far formal childcare services are able to meet the needs of these parents. This study focuses particularly on the barriers to developing such services, and on what might help. It draws on a survey of all English EYDCPs in 2002, surveys of national childcare organisations and childcare providers, and case studies of services offering atypical hours childcare.

Outline of the report

We begin the presentation of findings from the study by looking at the demand for atypical hours childcare (Chapter 2) before turning to consider the barriers and facilitators to service development, using examples drawn from the case studies (Chapter 3). In conclusion, we draw out the implications from the study for policy and service development (Chapter 4).

2

The demand for atypical hours childcare

This chapter looks at the need for childcare at atypical times, the source of demand and whether and how this demand is met. It is important to note, however, the difficulties of assessing demand for childcare services. Accurate, reliable information is not easily obtained. EYDCPs may undertake surveys of local parents as part of their childcare audits, but response rates to such questionnaires are usually extremely low, and responses are difficult to interpret (Moss et al, 1998). Children's Information Services (CISs)[1] in some authorities follow up all enquiries about childcare and collect information on whether parents found a provider, but even this method cannot provide a comprehensive picture of demand and unmet demand. Not every parent contacts a CIS, and of those who do, only a minority will return monitoring forms. A more fundamental difficulty in assessing demand in order to plan and develop services is that parents make choices in a particular context:

"While parents appeared generally happy with their choice of informal and/or parental childcare, it was nevertheless a choice that might have been made in a context where formal and affordable childcare options were not available. However, this complex scenario makes it difficult to predict the type, nature and amount of additional formal provision that would be necessary to fill the gaps identified by the study". (La Valle et al, 2002, p 62)

Demand for childcare services depends on circumstances, and will be affected by a whole range of factors such as the cost of care, parents' incomes, the quality of services on offer, and more intangible factors such as cultural attitudes and the acceptability of different forms of childcare at different times.

Extent of demand

In our study, we drew on three sources of information to consider the extent of demand for childcare at atypical times: EYDCPs, national childcare organisations, and childcare providers. Bearing in mind the caveats discussed above, the overall consensus was that there was a limited demand, rather than a significant one, for childcare at atypical times. None of the EYDCPs reported that there was *no* demand for childcare outside standard working hours[2], although a few did not know. On the other hand, only 10% rated this demand as significant. The great

Table 2.1: Demand for atypical hours childcare, as reported by EYDCPs

Extent of demand	% of EYDCPs
Significant	10
Some	74
Little	13
None	0
Don't know	3
Base = 114	

---

[1] Each local authority has a CIS which holds the database of registered providers in their area and provides information to parents on childcare. The CIS also provides statistical information for the childcare audit that each EYDCP has to undertake every three years.

[2] Defined for the purpose of this study as outside Monday to Friday, 8am to 6pm, or childcare needed at times that vary.

Table 2.2: Times when childcare at atypical times is mostly required, as reported by EYDCPs

Time	% of EYDCPs[a]
After 6pm	70
At times that vary	62
Before 8am	54
Weekends	45
Overnight	13
Don't know	7
Base = 113	

[a] Respondents could list up to three choices.

majority thought that there was 'some' demand, with the rest describing little demand for such provision (Table 2.1).

Based mainly on information from their members, national childcare organisations felt that the demand tended to be for evenings and weekends and less for overnight care. Both the National Childminding Association (NCMA) and National Day Nurseries Association (NDNA) considered the demand to be strongest for childcare that extended by an hour or so beyond standard hours, often to cover commuting times. This was also the perception of the EYDCPs, although they considered there was also a demand for childcare at times that varied. Less than one in eight perceived a need for overnight care (Table 2.2).

The survey of providers revealed a similar picture of some unmet demand from parents for childcare at atypical times, and particularly for childcare in the evenings and at times that vary (Table 2.3). Childminders were more likely than other types of provider to accommodate childcare in the early morning and at times that vary, and therefore reported less of an unmet demand for these times. However, similar proportions of childminders and day nurseries had been asked to provide care in the evening, but had been either unable or unwilling to do so. There was little reported demand for care overnight and at weekends: 85% of providers said that they had never been asked to do this on a regular basis.

Other surveys of parents' childcare needs suggest that there is a demand for formal services generally (although the difficulty in establishing demand needs to be kept in mind), and that some parents working non-standard hours have difficulties in finding suitable childcare. For example, in the second survey for the DfES of parents' demand for childcare (Woodland et al, 2002) less than half of working mothers used formal childcare in the past year, but when the whole sample of working mothers were asked about this, 85% indicated that they would like to use formal childcare if it was readily available and affordable. This survey also revealed that unsuitable working hours was a reason for not working outside the home for a quarter of mothers in two-parent families and just over a third of lone mothers. However, only 6% and 5% respectively gave unsocial work hours as a reason, although unsocial work hours were not defined. Despite this, a quarter of those parents who were working and who started before 8am or finished after 6pm said that these non-standard hours caused them problems with their childcare arrangements. Sixteen per cent of all parents in the survey felt that providers could improve the range of hours they were open for. Focus groups of parents in the DfES study on atypical hours and childcare were also

Table 2.3: Number of providers reporting unmet demand for childcare at atypical times

Been asked, but unable or unwilling to provide childcare	CM	DN	OOS	PG	ALL	
	n	n	n	n	n	%
Before 8am	21	11	3	3	38	12
Between 6pm and 8pm	49	8	3	1	61	20
At times that vary	21	14	3	4	42	13
Overnight	28	0	3	1	32	10
Weekend	29	1	3	1	34	11
Base	212	41	35	23	312	

Note: CM=childminders, DN=day nurseries, OOS=out-of-school services, PG=pre-school playgroups.

dissatisfied with the hours that childcare providers offered (DfES, 2001a).

Source of demand

The employment sectors which particularly require staff to work atypical hours include public services providing 24-hour cover, seven days a week such as the NHS, police, fire and prison services; retail distribution, banking and the finance sector; manufacturing; leisure and tourism (DfES 2001a). National childcare organisations in our study, when asked to identify where the demand came from, mentioned both the 'traditional' service industries such as the NHS, but also referred to call centres, the media and transport. Demand may also ebb and flow, as in seasonal employment in the tourist industry, which makes assessing demand more difficult.

Several of the childcare organisation representatives to whom we spoke thought that demand for childcare at atypical times mostly comes from disadvantaged areas where proportionally more parents work non-standard hours than in more advantaged areas. However, the study undertaken by La Valle et al (2002) shows no clear link between atypical hours and qualifications or skill levels among mothers, although there was a clearer link for fathers. Control over working arrangements was related to parents' labour market position, with those in lower socioeconomic groups more likely than those in professional jobs to feel that they had no choice other than to work atypical hours.

Meeting demand

Only two EYDCPs in our survey thought that the demand for atypical hours childcare was currently being met. Seventy per cent thought it was partly met, 18% that it was not met at all, and the remainder did not know. Relatives and friends played a major role in providing such care (Table 2.4). Parents who frequently work atypical hours are more likely than others to use informal childcare when they work, either because this is their preferred option or because of a lack of affordable childcare (DfES, 2001a; La Valle et al, 2002).

Table 2.4: Main providers of atypical hours childcare, as reported by EYDCPs (%)

Type of service	EYDCPs
Informal (eg relatives)	37
Formal childcare	6
Mix of formal and informal	57

Base = 84

Outside of standard working hours, formal services were most likely to offer childcare before 8am and after 6pm, and much less likely to cover weekends, overnight stays or irregular hours (Table 2.5). Childminders were the most common providers of atypical hours care, but even so, less than half of EYDCPs thought that more than a few childminders offered this service (Table 2.6). The DfES study (2001a) also found that EYDCPs often knew of only one or two providers that offered care at atypical times.

Table 2.5: EYDCPs reporting services covering atypical hours in their area (%)

	CM	DN	OOS	PG
Before 8am	84	61	46	6
After 6pm	80	33	23	1
At times that vary	60	7	3	0
Weekend	58	18	13	1
Overnight	50	4	0	0
Don't know	3	3	4	7

Base = 114

Note: CM=childminders, DN=day nurseries, OOS=out-of-school services, PG=pre-school playgroups.

Table 2.6: Extent of providers offering atypical hours childcare, as reported by EYDCPs (%)

	CM	DN	OOS	PG
Many	4	4	3	1
Some	33	12	9	1
Few	55	47	37	6
None	2	16	21	54
Don't know	6	21	30	38

Base = 114

Note: CM=childminders, DN=day nurseries, OOS=out-of-school services, PG=pre-school playgroups.

These findings are mirrored in our survey of childcare providers. We asked providers what was the earliest time of day they *regularly* cared for a child from, as a formal arrangement rather than on an occasional basis, and the latest time a child could regularly stay until (Table 2.7). Childminders were the most likely to offer childcare outside standard working hours. Around a half took children before 8am and nearly a quarter provided care after 6pm, although this flexibility usually extended to only an hour earlier or later. Around one in three of both day nurseries and out-of-school services accepted children before 8am and about one in 10 kept them after 6pm, but none of these services offered care before 7am or after 7pm. Pre-school playgroups were very unlikely to operate a service covering even standard working hours.

There are, of course, a number of particular difficulties that pre-school playgroups face if they want to offer childcare at atypical times. These groups have traditionally offered sessional care, for two to three hours either in the morning or afternoon. Furthermore, they have relied on parents to help run and staff them. Often they are accommodated in church halls or community centres. For these reasons, they have generally not provided a childcare service for working parents. Over recent years and encouraged by the National Childcare Strategy, some pre-school playgroups have begun to extend their opening hours. However, according to the Pre-School Learning Alliance (PLA), expansion of this service is hampered by lack of facilities and limited funding. A recent survey of 16,000 pre-school playgroups affiliated to the PLA found that more than eight in 10 (83%) do not own their own premises and almost three quarters (73%) are not the sole users of their pre-school premises and have to share facilities (Tweed, 2002). Although some PLA members do open at 7.30am and some close at 7pm, persuading members to extend hours to cover standard rather than atypical working hours remains the PLA focus.

None of the childcare providers in our survey offered care before 6.45am or after 9pm. Asked if they had ever provided childcare outside standard hours, a small proportion of childminders said that they had regularly cared for children overnight (8%) and at weekends (6%), but none were currently doing so, and none of the other types of service had ever done this.

"I used to provide childcare for an 8-year-old from 6.30am on some shifts, the other end would be pick-up from school and have [child] until 10.30pm. In this case I would go to [child's] house, they would have a bath and be able to go to bed as normal. I would have [child] once every three weeks on a Saturday morning. The family moved from the area so I no longer do this." (Childminder)

Over half of childminders and nearly a quarter of day nurseries and out-of-school services had, however, taken children at times that varied from week to week (Table 2.8).

Table 2.7: Times childcare currently offered by each provider type

	CM	DN	OOS	PG	ALL	
	n	n	n	n	n	%
Before 7am	1	0	0	0	1	<1
Before 8am	111	11	14	1	137	42
After 6pm	49	4	3	0	56	17
After 7pm	1	0	0	0	1	<1
Base	218	42	40	24	324	

Note: CM=childminders, DN=day nurseries, OOS=out-of-school services, PG=pre-school playgroups.

Table 2.8: Number of providers having ever regularly provided childcare outside standard hours

	CM	DN	OOS	PG	ALL	
	n	n	n	n	n	%
Before 8am	140	14	13	2	169	54
Between 6pm and 8pm	35	2	1	0	38	12
Overnight	15	0	0	0	15	5
Weekend	12	1	0	0	13	4
At times that vary	120	9	8	3	140	45
Base	212	41	35	23	312	

Note: CM=childminders, DN=day nurseries, OOS=out-of-school services, PG=pre-school playgroups.

Providers' willingness to work atypical hours

Providers were asked about their willingness to regularly work outside their current working hours (that is, to alter their starting and finishing times). It should be noted that almost two thirds (65%) already started between 7.30 and up to and *including* 8am and finished between 5.30 and 6pm. Over a third were willing to consider regularly working outside their usual working hours, although only 7% were definite that they would do this and well over half were not willing to at all (Table 2.9). Pre-school playgroup leaders were more likely than other types of service provider to be prepared to work outside their usual hours, although our sample is small. Since playgroup sessions usually last only two to three hours, their willingness to extend their hours is perhaps not surprising, but they are unlikely to provide childcare at times that would meet the needs of parents working atypical hours.

In another question, providers were asked about their willingness to provide childcare in the early morning (before 8am), in the late evening (up to 8pm), overnight, at the weekend and at times that varied from week to week. Half of providers were willing to provide childcare in the early morning and 41% at times that varied from week to week. However, less than one in ten said that they would be willing to care for children in the late evening and very few (3-4%) were willing to provide care overnight or at the weekend (Tables 2.10-2.15).

Table 2.9: Number of providers willing to work outside their current working hours

	CM	DN	OOS	PG	ALL	
	n	*n*	*n*	*n*	*n*	*%*
Yes	17	1	2	4	24	*7*
Maybe	65	16	13	7	101	*31*
No	136	23	17	13	189	*58*
Don't know	3	2	5	0	10	*3*
Base	221	42	37	24	324	

Note: CM=childminders, DN=day nurseries, OOS=out-of-school services, PG=pre-school playgroups.

Table 2.10: Providers' willingness to provide childcare at specific atypical times (%)

	Yes	Maybe	No	Don't know	Base
Before 8am	50	14	34	2	315
Up to 8pm	9	19	71	1	312
Overnight	3	15	79	3	311
Weekends	4	12	80	4	312
Times that vary	41	21	35	2	314

Table 2.11: Number of providers of each type willing to provide childcare *before 8am*

	CM	DN	OOS	PG
Yes	125	16	12	3
Maybe	29	7	7	1
No	60	15	14	19
Don't know	0	3	2	1
Base	214	41	35	24

Note: CM=childminders, DN=day nurseries, OOS=out-of-school services, PG=pre-school playgroups.

Table 2.12: Number of providers of each type willing to provide childcare *up to 8pm*

	CM	DN	OOS	PG
Yes	23	2	1	1
Maybe	40	9	7	3
No	149	28	25	19
Don't know	1	1	1	1
Base	213	40	34	24

Note: CM=childminders, DN=day nurseries, OOS=out-of-school services, PG=pre-school playgroups.

Table 2.13: Number of providers of each type willing to provide childcare *overnight*

	CM	DN	OOS	PG
Yes	9	0	0	0
Maybe	37	5	4	1
No	159	35	29	22
Don't know	6	1	1	1
Base	211	41	34	24

Note: CM=childminders, DN=day nurseries, OOS=out-of-school services, PG=pre-school playgroups.

Table 2.14: Number of providers of each type willing to provide childcare *at the weekend*

	CM	DN	OOS	PG
Yes	11	1	0	0
Maybe	28	5	4	1
No	169	32	27	22
Don't know	6	2	2	1
Base	214	40	33	24

Note: CM=childminders, DN=day nurseries, OOS=out-of-school services, PG=pre-school playgroups.

Table 2.15: Number of providers of each type willing to provide childcare *at times that vary*

	CM	DN	OOS	PG
Yes	114	6	5	4
Maybe	43	12	9	2
No	56	19	19	17
Don't know	2	2	2	1
Base	215	39	35	24

"We are open 8am to 6pm and very busy. I find running a day nursery, and staffing it in particular, around these hours [is] difficult enough. Anything more would ruin my personal family life." (Day nursery)

"I have a young family of my own and feel that evenings/weekends are family time. My children already share me during the week." (Childminder)

The reasons why providers were unwilling to provide childcare during these times are explored in greater depth in the next chapter, but included their attitudes concerning the appropriateness of non-parental childcare at atypical times and the impact on their own family life of working atypical hours.

It appears that more providers say they are willing to provide childcare that covers non-standard hours than say they will work outside their usual working times. This is not as contradictory as it might at first appear, since 43% of providers were already providing childcare *before* 8am, while 18% provided childcare after 6pm (see Table 2.7).

Within these figures, there were some differences between provider types (Tables 2.11 – 2.15). Childminders were the most likely to be prepared to provide childcare at each of the specified atypical times, ranging from over half (58%) who were willing to provide childcare before 8am, down to just 4% who were prepared to provide care overnight. Playgroups were the least likely group to be willing to offer care at atypical times, apart from at times that varied from week to week. Day nurseries and out-of-school services came inbetween, with over a third willing to provide care before 8am and a much smaller number willing to do so at other atypical times. However, other providers in our survey indicated that they would 'maybe' consider offering care at such times, reinforcing the need to explore the barriers that are preventing them from doing so and the factors that influence their decision. This is the focus of our next chapter.

Summary

There is some demand for childcare outside the working hours of 8am to 6pm, Monday to Friday, but it appears limited, especially for overnight care. However, it is difficult to make an accurate estimate of demand because many parents will have already made arrangements and/or are not aware that formal childcare could be an option at these times. Most EYDCPs believe that existing demand is partly rather than fully met, mostly by informal care providers such as partners, relatives and friends. Most childminders do provide care in the early morning, but this is unlikely to be before 7am, and very few offer care after 7pm or at weekends. Other types of childcare service were even less likely to offer atypical hours care. Providers were more willing to provide childcare in the early morning and at times that varied from week to week. While over a third of providers were willing to consider regularly working outside their current working hours, this rarely extended to late evenings, overnight or at weekends.

3

Developing services to meet atypical work times

In this chapter, we consider how services are being developed to meet the needs of parents working at atypical times. Using data from our case studies, surveys of EYDCPs and providers, and interviews with national childcare organisations, we look at both the barriers to service development and what has or would facilitate development. But first we provide a thumb-nail sketch of each of the case studies:

- an NHS Trust Children's Centre in London
- a Community Nanny Scheme in Yorkshire
- a nanny working for the scheme in Yorkshire
- an NHS Trust Childminding Network, Saturday Club and Sitter Service in Birmingham
- a Childminding Network in Avon and Somerset
- a childminder working for a third network.

Abacus Children's Centre, University Hospital, Lewisham

In July 2002, the Abacus Children's Centre, which was open from 7am to 6pm, began offering childcare during the evenings and at weekends. An extension to the Centre's building in the grounds of the hospital was added to accommodate this service, which means that children attending during the evenings and weekends use their own dedicated space. Evening sessions are from 6pm to 10pm, and the centre opens from 7am to 6pm on Saturdays and Sundays. The local Trust has set up a 'bank' of 15 nursery nurses for evening and weekend working, which operates in the same way as a nursing 'bank' (a register of qualified nurses who can be offered work on a sessional basis).

The service is available to all posts and grades within the NHS Trust and is being extended to outside users in order to increase use. When there is sufficient demand for the service among Trust employees, use by non-employees will be phased out. Parents must book evening and weekend childcare seven days in advance, unless it is an emergency, such as a breakdown in usual childcare arrangements.

The service can take 12 children aged from three months to 12 years, although in practice the oldest child to attend has been eight years old. To date, there has been no demand from parents with older children. Fees are calculated on a sliding scale and parents pay a little more for evening and weekend care. For the under twos, parents on the highest incomes pay £23 for four hours in the evening, while those on a low income pay £18 (in 2002).

Development of this service took over a year and was prompted by management requests for childcare that supported the needs of their workforce operating a 24/7 service. The Trust recognised that good quality childcare was essential for parents to work effectively in the knowledge that their children were safe and well cared for. Furthermore, such a service offered flexible childcare to parents and supported recruitment and retention, as well as initiatives to improve working lives. The Trust received funding through the NHS Childcare Strategy, which enabled the Centre to expand and to develop innovative ideas for childcare.

Bradford Community Nanny Scheme

Gingerbread

In 1998-99, Bradford EYDCP's childcare audit identified a gap in the supply of childcare for lone parents working non-standard hours. Gingerbread (a charity supporting lone parents) together with the EYDCP and Registration and Inspection Unit (R&I) in Bradford Social Services discussed the possibility of organising a scheme modelled on the Dundee Sitter Scheme (Daycare Trust, 2000) and a fact-finding visit to the Dundee scheme was arranged. The EYDCP agreed to fund a coordinator's post for a year, which was filled in January 2001.

The Bradford Community Nanny Scheme started in March 2002 and offers childcare seven days a week from 7am to 10pm for lone-parent families. Parental fees are set on a sliding scale related to earnings, although most parents are on low incomes. The cost of the service is £18 an hour, but the most parents are required to pay is £6 an hour. The community nannies employed by the scheme provide childcare in the child's home. The scheme is not just for working parents, but also provides respite care and care for emergencies and for parents who are training or studying. The project receives referrals from social services.

Seven nannies currently work for the scheme and all are qualified nursery nurses. The nannies are employed as casual workers, working as and when required and being paid on an hourly rate. All have agreed to work atypical hours, but do have some choice about their hours. For example, a parent wanted a nanny between 8pm and 9pm, but the only nanny with spare capacity did not accept the 'job' because it would have meant two hours' travelling for one hour's work.

When a parent makes an initial enquiry, the coordinator establishes eligibility (lone parent), when and why they want childcare and where they live (the nanny would need to live within a reasonable proximity to the family). The coordinator makes a home visit accompanied by the nanny in order to meet the family and complete the registration form, contract, and financial and home safety assessments. The project has a small grant to provide equipment and toys on loan.

Fourteen families currently use the service and the amount of care varies from three to 15 hours a week for each family. The scheme is full and has a waiting list. Parents would like more hours and it is clear that demand is only partially met. It is also clear that there is a need for such a service for two-parent families, from whom they get many enquiries. For six of the 14 families, the service is being used so that they can take up work, but many are using the scheme as a 'top-up' to other childcare or early years services. In these circumstances, nannies will often take children to, or collect them from, other services or a relative.

Although the project is funded to provide 90 hours of childcare a week, in practice these are rarely all used as a parent may cancel or a nanny may be unavailable through sickness. Most months, a number of hours are carried forward. The coordinator tries to keep five hours a week 'floating' so that there is some spare capacity for emergency requests, although again the ability to respond depends on when the childcare is needed and if there is a nanny available to do the hours.

The scheme offers several benefits to lone parents including: convenience because the carer comes to the children; continuity in terms of a child's routines; childcare that is affordable because it is charged per household, not per child; flexibility in that it can be used for irregular childcare needs.

A community nanny

Kath Jarvis works for the Bradford Community Nanny Scheme. She qualified as a nursery nurse 16 years ago, then aged 41. She first worked in a community centre running the crèche and parent/toddler group, but moved to a private day nursery when, after nine years, she was made redundant. She worked at the nursery for six years and by the time she left was the officer-in-charge. She had been working full time, as much as 48 to 50 hours a week, and was working her notice when she saw the advertisement for the community nanny.

At the time of the interview for this study, Kath was working on average 24 to 25 hours a week. It has taken some time for her hours to build up, as parents joining the scheme needed to be 'matched' with the hours nannies could work. As with the other six nannies in the scheme, her contract states that working hours are between the hours of 7am and 10pm and may include weekends. In practice, she has only occasionally worked until 8.30pm. Her preference is not to work at weekends, but she has done the odd Sunday afternoon. Nannies are paid for the hours they work and are employed as sessional workers. This means that they are not eligible for paid leave, which was made clear at the time of recruitment. Travelling expenses are paid for the second and subsequent journeys in a day (the first is seen as the journey from home to work), but journey time is not paid.

Kath is currently providing childcare to six different families and the children she cares for range in age from 10 months to 12 years, although the majority are five or under. Her working week before the interview was:

Monday	7.15am - 9.00am	(Family 1)
	10.30am - 1.30pm	(Family 2)
Tuesday	9.30am - 12.00am	(Family 3)
Wednesday	8.15am - 1.00pm	(Family 4)
	2.00pm - 5.00pm	(Family 5)
Thursday	7.15am - 9.00am	(Family 1)
	1.30pm - 4.00pm	(Meeting at Gingerbread)
	6.30pm - 9.00pm	(Evening course which Kath is paid to attend)
Friday	9.30am - 5.00pm	(Family 6)

Kath enjoys working as a community nanny. Compared to the nursery, she likes the greater variety in terms of place of work, age group of the children and working on her own, although with support. Much trust is needed between a parent and nanny for the relationship to be successful. Although the nanny who will be working with the family accompanies the coordinator on the first visit, this may be the only opportunity they have to meet parent and child before the childcare begins. They may not meet the child at all, especially if they are at school. Parents are often desperate for childcare in order to start work, which means that there is no chance for a settling-in period, as might occur in a nursery or with a childminder. If the childcare is only for a short period each week, it can take time to build up a relationship with parent and/or child.

A record book is kept with every parent for nannies to record what they have done, for example activities, nappy changes, meals, and so on. Parents can also add comments. This is important because nannies and parents might not meet up, for example when the nanny takes a child to nursery school and the parent collects.

Childminding Network, Saturday Club and Sitter Service

Sandwell and West Birmingham NHS Trust

Sandwell and West Birmingham NHS Trust had for some time been discussing how best to meet the childcare needs of employees working shifts. There was already a well-established workplace nursery with opening hours from 7.30am to 6pm. Although the nursery could have opened earlier to accommodate those starting work at 6am, this would not have helped parents working 2pm to 10pm or 10pm to 6am shifts. In considering what was best for children, they felt that extending the opening hours of the nursery was not the way forward, since children could be in the nursery not only overnight, but most of the day while the parent slept. Instead, childminders were thought to be a good alternative because they could provide a home-like environment.

The *Childminding Network* has taken two years to develop and it is only since August 2002 that it has been promoted by the Trust. The network is managed by the Trust and the Trust's childcare coordinator is the network coordinator, although a replacement was being sought at the time of interview. The network coordinator's role is to support network childminders, assure quality and be a point of contact for parents. In order to obtain funding from the EYDCP, the network had to offer childcare to the community and not just NHS staff.

There are currently 10 childminders in the network, but the aim is to increase this to 20. Childminders joining the network must have a childcare qualification (for example Diploma in Childminding Practice or National Vocational Qualification) because this is considered important in assuring quality. This means that network childminders have usually been childminding for at least a year. Childminders joining the network do not have to agree to work atypical hours. For example, one childminder works 8.30am to 5.30pm three days a week because this suits her circumstances. The childcare needs of the NHS workforce are diverse and such hours may for example suit a part-time administrative worker. Currently the network has no members regularly working late evenings or weekends or providing overnight care, although most have indicated that they would be willing to do so. Childminders are self-employed and determine the fees they will charge themselves, although the fee is often negotiated with parents.

The *Saturday Club* developed following a staff survey, which indicated demand for the nursery to open at weekends, but for older as well as younger children. In order not to deter older children from attending, the service was called a Saturday Club, although it is held in the nursery. The club opens from 8.30am until 5pm and has 22 places for children aged between three months and 12 years. Different age groups occupy different space in the nursery. The Trust is prepared to extend the service to Sunday if there is demand. Parents pay £15 for the day for each child.

The *Sitter Service* is in the early stages of planning. The nursery has a bank of nursery nurses, many of whom would welcome the opportunity to work more hours. The idea is to register a sitter service where nursery nurses would provide childcare in the child's home. The idea has been well received by parents, although they have stressed that they would want staff they knew, 'not strangers'.

The Avon and Somerset Police Constabulary Childminding Network

Having received some funding to develop childcare services with employers, the National Childminding Association's (NCMA) Development Officer for the South West of England successfully negotiated with Avon and Somerset Police Constabulary (ASPC) the contract for this network.

The contract pays for a part-time network coordinator and the training needs of the network. Not only does the coordinator recruit, support and monitor the quality of network childminders, but she is also a point of contact for any parent employed by the Constabulary wanting help with childcare. Only one parent needs to be an employee and there is no differentiation on the grounds of gender or rank nor whether civilian or police. If necessary, the coordinator can put parents in touch with a network childminder who is convenient in terms of location. Should there be no vacancies with childminders in the network or no one in a convenient location for the parent, the coordinator can approach childminders belonging to other networks to see if they would be willing to provide childcare. The coordinator updates the vacancies among childminders in the network on a monthly basis and has vacancy information from the coordinators of the other eight networks within the Fourways area (which covers four local authorities).

There are currently 10 childminders in the network, but the aim is to increase this to 20. Under the contract, the network offers 20 places to ASPC employees, although this will take time to achieve as places become available when children currently with the childminders leave. Ideally, network childminders should keep one or two places available for police employees, but in practice this may not be possible because there is no financial help such as a retainer.

The network offers childcare to cover both standard and non-standard working hours. In joining the network, childminders therefore agreed to work shift patterns, including overnight and weekend care if necessary. Although registration for overnight care was not a condition of acceptance to the network, all childminders were made aware that parents could want overnight care and that they would need to be registered for this.

The network is very much in its infancy and at the time of interview no childminder provided childcare for ASPC employees. Enquiries from parents continue to increase as the network is marketed. Most enquiries have been for standard hours (8am to 6pm), although one parent has indicated that she would require overnight care if she is promoted as her partner also works shifts. One difficulty is that because the area is so large, the coordinator does not know where childcare may be needed. The other factor is that demand takes time to build while parents become aware that formal childcare is a real option at atypical times.

In addition to their OFSTED registration and annual inspection, each childminder interested in joining the network must participate in 'Children Come First', the quality assurance scheme administered by the NCMA. They must reach the required standards of quality to be accepted for the network. To assure quality following the initial assessment, an unannounced visit is made once a term by the network coordinator, who also undertakes a monitoring visit every six to eight weeks. Network childminders and the coordinator work together to identify training needs and how best to accommodate them. The contract with ASPC includes a training budget for network childminders.

A network childminder

Ann Ford has been a childminder for three years and has been offering childcare covering atypical hours since she started childminding. She will provide childcare between 6am and 7pm, Monday to Friday, and 8.30am to 6pm at the weekends. She is currently working from 7.50am to 6.30pm during the week and every other Saturday from 8.30am to 1.30pm. In addition to her childminding, she also provides respite care and was until recently working on Sundays from 8.30am to 6pm. She cannot provide overnight care because she has no space for another bed. Ann charges no more than her daily rate of £2.50 an hour for childcare before 8am or after 6pm, but increases her rate to £3 an hour for weekend care.

Ann was prepared to work at atypical times because she recognised that childcare does not start and end at regular times and that parents often do not have a choice about working atypical hours. She was keen to provide respite care because having a child with a disability herself she would have welcomed this sort of help when he was younger.

She has not experienced any problems with combining childcare covering both standard and non-standard hours, although she has found it a little easier to match children to childcare 'slots' the longer she has been childminding. Ann believes it is important to be sensitive to children's needs at whatever time they attend.

It should be emphasised that most of these services are very new, although the process of setting them up may have been taking place for some considerable time. At the time of the interview with the Saturday Club, for example, it had been open two months – only eight times. The childminding networks were also very new and none of the members were yet providing atypical hours childcare. All the services gave permission for their details to be included in this report.

In the rest of this chapter, we draw on information from these case studies, the interviews with national childcare organisations and the surveys of EYDCPs and childcare providers, to illustrate issues around developing childcare services to meet the needs of parents working atypical hours.

The role of EYDCPs and childcare organisations in service development

The general view among the six national childcare organisations was that there was a need to develop services in this area. However, some were not actively encouraging their membership to do so because they were not convinced that childcare at atypical times was in the best interest of children. We return to this issue in more detail in the section on 'children's welfare' later in this chapter. None of the provider organisations had so far developed official policies in this area, perhaps reflecting the drive to expand childcare services to cover standard working hours, rather than atypical hours.

Most representatives of the 114 EYDCPs surveyed (85%) thought that there was a need to develop or further develop childcare services for those working atypical hours. Almost all the rest (13%) did not know. However, less than one in three had tried to do so, with another third planning this for the future. Those who had attempted to develop atypical hours provision described a variety of approaches, including:

- encouraging existing providers, especially childminders, to consider extending their hours or to develop flexible arrangements;
- recruitment campaigns to attract new childcare workers who would be willing to provide care out of hours, at weekends or on an ad hoc basis;
- offering grants to childminders to provide overnight and extended hours services;
- developing provision through childminder networks;
- working with schools to set up breakfast and after-school clubs;
- supporting a nursery that wanted to open on Saturdays.

Table 3.1: Difficulties faced by EYDCPs in developing childcare services covering atypical times (%)

Difficulties	EYDCPs
Not tried to develop such provision yet	41
Childcare workers' reluctance to work non-standard hours	49
Financial (eg sustainability, funding, costs)	38
Unpredictability of hours required	36
Lack of interest or support from employers	26
Lack of government encouragement and guidance	21
Planning requirements	16
Providing continuity of care	15
Other	11

Base = 110

Table 3.2: What has helped those EYDCPs who were developing atypical hours childcare services (%)

Helped	EYDCPs
Providers wanting to offer this service	63
Ability to offer financial support	41
Significant demand for the service	39
Suitable premises	29
Support from employers	25
Government encouragement and guidance	23
Examples of good practice from other EYDCPs	16
Other	14

Base = 56

Barriers and what would help in developing services

Where EYDCPs had tried to develop atypical hours childcare, the most common difficulty they had faced was the reluctance of childcare workers to work non-standard hours, followed by financial considerations such as sustainability, funding and costs. Over a third mentioned the unpredictability of hours required, and just over a quarter said service development had been hampered by the lack of interest or support shown by employers. We return to the question of employer support in the concluding chapter. Less frequently mentioned barriers included lack of government encouragement and guidance, planning requirements and the difficulty of ensuring continuity of care for children (Table 3.1).

When EYDCPs were asked what had been most helpful in enabling them to develop services, the factors they identified were the reverse of those that had created the most difficulties. The most important factor was having providers who wanted to offer the service, and the ability to offer them financial support, for example, through the National Opportunity Fund (NOF), childminding start-up grants or the Neighbourhood Nurseries Initiative. It clearly helped if there was a demand for atypical hours care. A number of rural partnerships commented that childcare services in rural areas faced particular problems because of the scattered population and lack of sufficient demand. One

partnership representative commented:"The rural nature of [our area] makes any viable childcare difficult. The low demand for atypical hours simply exacerbates this". Other factors that helped were employer support and the availability of suitable premises. Around a quarter of partnerships credited the government's encouragement and guidance with helping them to develop atypical hours childcare services, and a few had been assisted by examples of good practice from other partnerships (Table 3.2).

We saw in the previous chapter how providers are generally unwilling to work outside their usual working hours and are particularly reluctant to work late evenings or at the weekend. Providers were given a list of 13 possible barriers to providing childcare at atypical times and asked to indicate all that applied to them (Table 3.3). Almost three quarters said that they did not want to work these hours themselves and around a quarter that they could not get staff to work at these times. More than three quarters felt that working at atypical times would not be fair on their family. Other barriers, mentioned by between a third and a quarter of providers, included parents not being able to afford increased fees, registration requirements for overnight care, unsuitable premises, not knowing when children will attend and financial viability. Around a third of providers also believed that formal childcare at these hours was not necessarily good for children.

When we asked about what would help, around half of providers, especially childminders, said nothing would encourage them to offer childcare covering non-standard hours care; they just did not want to do it (Table 3.4). A third of childminders would be encouraged to offer atypical hours care if they could charge a higher fee, and over a third of day nurseries and out-of-school services thought that a subsidy or financial incentive would help, as well as more parents asking for this service. Day nurseries saw the greatest need as being able to offer better working conditions and recruit staff willing to work atypical hours. Around one in five of the group day care services (day nurseries, pre-school playgroups and out-of-school clubs), but hardly any childminders, thought that encouragement and guidance from the government and EYDCPs would facilitate the provision of childcare covering non-standard hours. Very few thought that a publicity campaign through newspapers or television would help to develop this service, suggesting the need for a more tailored personal approach.

Table 3.3: Number of providers identifying barriers to childcare at atypical times

	CM	DN	OOS	PG	ALL	
	n	*n*	*n*	*n*	*n*	*%*
Not fair on my own family	182	23	22	13	240	77
Do not want to work these hours myself	157	25	22	16	220	71
Children need their families during these times	72	22	14	9	117	37
Parents cannot afford increased fees	56	11	18	8	93	30
Registration requirements for overnight care	53	20	12	7	92	29
Hard to find staff to work these hours	7	**34**	23	16	80	26
Premises not suitable	36	14	15	15	80	26
Need to know when children will attend	38	18	13	7	76	24
Difficult to break even financially (low demand)	18	23	19	7	67	21
Increased insurance premium	15	14	11	7	47	15
Lack of support/interest from employers	3	9	8	4	24	8
Different skills needed for care at these times	4	7	3	2	16	5
Lack of guidance from government or EYDCP	6	5	2	2	15	5
Some other reason	7	5	7	2	21	7
Base	210	41	37	24	312	

Notes: CM=childminders, DN=day nurseries, OOS=out-of-school services, PG=pre-school playgroups.
Bold numbers indicate barriers mentioned by over 50% of respondents of that type of provider.

Table 3.4: Number of providers identifying what would encourage them to offer childcare at atypical times

	CM	DN	OOS	PG	ALL	
	n	*n*	*n*	*n*	*n*	*%*
Nothing – don't want to do it	121	15	17	13	166	54
Ability to charge a higher fee	69	12	11	3	95	31
Subsidy or financial incentive	45	14	15	8	82	26
More parents asking for this service	29	18	16	6	69	22
Being convinced that children will benefit	27	16	8	3	54	17
Staff willing to work at atypical times	2	22	12	9	45	15
Suitable premises	20	9	11	8	48	15
Better working conditions for staff	2	24	12	6	44	14
Government or EYDCP encouragement/guidance	9	9	7	5	30	10
Publicity campaign	9	2	4	2	17	6
Something else	9	3	2	0	14	5
Base	209	41	36	24	310	

Notes: CM=childminders, DN=day nurseries, OOS=out-of-school services, PG=pre-school playgroups.
Bold numbers indicate barriers mentioned by over 50% of respondents of that type of provider.

We take each of these barriers – reluctance of providers, parental demand, funding, viability and sustainability, registration and inspection, premises, support and training, and children's welfare – and discuss them in more detail.

Reluctance of providers to work at atypical times

We saw in the previous chapter that over half of all providers were not willing to consider working outside their usual working hours (Table 2.9). The reasons put forward for the reluctance of providers to work at atypical times included the impact on the provider's own family, the fact that many already work long hours, and the cost of the financial inducements perceived as necessary to attract providers to work these hours.

Impact on providers' families

Nearly 9 in 10 childminders, and over half of all other childcare services, believed it would not be fair on their family to provide atypical hours care:

"I feel it encroaches on the privacy of my other family members. My husband needs to unwind after long shifts. I also feel family time together is important and try to safeguard weekends for quality time together." (Childminder)

"The childcare I provide at the moment is for children of similar ages to my own children. These arrangements fit in well with my whole family. Personally I would not like to lose any of our 'family' time together or impose other children having to share bedrooms etc with my own children. I think this would be unfair." (Childminder)

It was not only the desire to protect 'family time' and meet the emotional needs of their families that was perceived as a barrier to working atypical hours, but also practical difficulties such as needing to provide care for their own children. Paid care has to be fitted around unpaid care, leading one nursery manager to remark that,"the system can only work if childcare for childcarers is established. As a parent, I find it difficult to ensure my child is collected from an after-school club by 6pm when I work until 6pm every night".

Although around a half of providers said nothing would encourage them to provide atypical hours childcare, the comments made by a number of childminders suggested that they might be prepared to offer such care at a later stage, when it fitted in better with their own family commitments.

"I have nothing against working outside standard hours in principle, but at the moment my children go to bed early and still need help feeding/dressing in the mornings, so I think they would suffer if I childminded during these times.... Most of the childminders I know are in a similar situation with small children on their own, which may be why there is a shortage of care during non-standard times?" (Childminder)

"Later on I would love to do short-term fostering and I wouldn't mind the different times." (Childminder)

This might suggest that to accommodate atypical hours childcare, childcare workers are more likely not to have childcare responsibilities themselves. Many of the Avon and Somerset network childminders were childless or had older children. Most of the community nannies did not have childcare responsibilities. Kath Jarvis, a community nanny, thought that someone thinking about this as a job should think about the hours involved:. "Being flexible in terms of availability is important and those with young children would probably find it difficult trying to fit it in around care of their own children". Although the NHS network coordinator thought it might be easier for childminders with older children to accommodate atypical hours, in practice the children of childminders in this network covered a wide age-span including pre-school children.

Working long hours: the logistics of combining standard and non-standard care

Providers were invited to comment at the end of the questionnaire and approximately one in five did so (18%). Many of the comments from childminders showed that they equated

21

providing childcare at atypical times with working a longer day. As many were already working 10 or more hours, they felt that this was not a realistic proposition, as the comments from these two childminders illustrate:

"Childminders would find it difficult doing non-standard hours for one child and ordinary working hours for others as we would be working far too many hours."

"I find the hours 8am to 5pm are as long as I can maintain giving quality standard to both my family and childminding."

Recruiting childminders to the NHS Trust Childminder's Network proved difficult initially, because childminders were reluctant to work late evenings or weekends, and overnight care meant re-registering to include care at this time. Their reluctance was due to several reasons, including the (mistaken) belief that they would have to be prepared to work at any hours to meet the needs of hospital staff, because the network was managed by the Trust. Childminders anticipated difficulties in combining the care of children across standard and non-standard hours, particularly since there is often an overlap. Filling childcare places so that the required adult:child ratio is maintained, while ensuring an adequate income is likely to be challenging. Yet it is possible. Ann Ford, who provided childcare at both standard and non-standard times, said it became a little easier to match children to places the more experienced one became. She worked 7.50am to 6.30pm, Monday to Friday, and 8.30am to 1.30pm on alternate weekends, and was prepared to start earlier. However, another childminder had had to reduce her care commitments to accommodate the unpredictable childcare needs of a lone parent who was a health service employee. Without this childminder, the parent would have found it difficult to work, but the childminder could only provide childcare at unpredictable times because she could afford not to take on other children.

Accommodating children across standard and non-standard times is not only an issue for childminders. In the NHS, the usual shift pattern for nurses is 2pm to 10pm, 10pm to 7am, and 7am to 2pm, but there is variation within these patterns and other groups of workers, such as catering and domestic staff, have different patterns. Since standard and non-standard hours care often overlap, the Children's Centre found that some juggling was required in order to accommodate parents' needs. For example, to accommodate a parent who wanted to use the Centre from 2pm to 10pm, a place would need to be available from 2pm to 6pm as well as 6pm to 10pm when the evening service operated.

Because of the possibility that childminders could be working very long hours, some thought that nurseries might be in a better position to offer non-standard hours care because staff could work shifts. But nearly all of nursery managers envisaged difficulty in finding staff prepared to work such hours:

"Finding quality staff is always difficult – to find staff who would be willing to work early or late would be even more so." (Day nursery)

"We are a nursery school. We are asked to provide childcare before 8.30am and after 4.15pm, but it is not possible to recruit staff for 'odd hours' and not enough interest from parents." (Nursery school).

Yet, the group-based providers among our case studies had little difficulty in recruiting staff for their service, and were able to find nursery nurses who wanted to work atypical hours. For some who had children of their own, working evenings and/or at the weekend meant that they could rely on a partner or relative to care for their children and thus avoid childcare costs. For others, as in the case of two of the four staff working at the Saturday Club, they wanted to work more hours to increase income. The Community Nanny Scheme likewise had little difficulty in recruiting nannies and the first round of recruitment met with a large response.

Financial incentives

National childcare organisations felt that childcare workers deserved a work–life balance themselves and that working atypical hours threatened this. They were of the opinion that financial incentives, such as premium rates for nursery staff and higher fees for childminders, were necessary to encourage childcare workers to work such hours. However, pay for the childcare workforce is at a low level to start with and higher rates may not be a sufficient incentive. Furthermore, higher staff costs are passed on to parents in increased fees. As pointed out by representatives of these organisations and around a third of providers, many parents cannot afford to pay more.

Since the Birmingham and Avon and Somerset childminding networks were so new, there was no information on the fees charged for atypical hours. Ann Ford, who worked for another network, increased her hourly rate of £2.50 by 50p for weekend care, but did not charge extra for care before 8am or after 6pm. Ann chose to work at atypical times partly in order to support parents, particularly lone parents, who often had no choice about working these times. Although parent and childminder together negotiate fees, one network coordinator felt that there were issues about what to charge, particularly for overnight care. It might not seem fair to charge a higher rate for a child who is asleep much of the time, but on the other hand, the childminder is working unsocial hours if the child wakes in the night.

As demonstrated by our case studies, childminder networks may be one way of encouraging childminders to offer atypical hours care. Childminders in a network benefit from the support of a coordinator, who helps in promoting business (for example the Birmingham and Avon and Somerset networks), ensures standards of quality and provides training opportunities. The Avon and Somerset network had little difficulty in recruiting childminders willing to work non-standard hours. They already had a pool of childminders waiting to join a network, some of whom were part of an existing network whose funding had ceased, and others who had looked after the children of Avon and Somerset Police Constabulary employees in the past. The NHS coordinator, having successfully obtained a grant from the EYDCP which was promoting outside play, was able to offer each childminder joining the NHS network a pack of outdoor equipment worth £250.

Although the bank of staff that worked in the Children's Centre were paid a little more for working unsocial hours, Saturday Club staff were not. The nannies in the Community Nanny Scheme were employed as casual workers, working as and when required on an hourly rate

irrespective of whether they were working standard or non-standard hours. Although the hourly rate may be higher than nursery nurses are paid in the private sector, nannies were not eligible for paid leave.

Demand, funding, viability and sustainability

Our study highlighted several issues to do with demand: the extent of demand (discussed in the Chapter 2); whether demand is sufficient to make providing atypical hours care worthwhile; and the time it can take demand to build up. Comments from EYDCP coordinators illustrate how take-up of a new service can be disappointing:

"We have tried breakfast clubs with little interest from parents."

"We opened one nursery on a Saturday but didn't have many places taken up, two to three each session."

"Had discussions with some nurseries asking them to consider offering weekend provision, but it's so ad hoc it's not been worth it."

This poor take-up could reflect the fact that in the absence of formal childcare services covering atypical working hours, most parents who need this type of care have made alternative informal arrangements and are reluctant to then move their child. Alternatively, it could reflect insufficient demand. The NHS childcare coordinator's experience shows how difficult it is to establish the real extent of demand. Despite many parents working night shifts, in three years she had received no requests for overnight care. She felt this was because parents were reluctant to use overnight childcare located outside the child's home or a relative's home. When a survey of staff suggested that there was a need for childcare over the Christmas period, they decided to open the nursery over Christmas at the usual fee. However, when they advised parents of this, most then said that they had made alternative arrangements.

Our case studies demonstrated how take-up is

slow and takes time to build up. Although the services had been operational for only a short time, the highest occupancy rate at the Children's Centre had been only 50% and at the Saturday Club 18%. The Saturday Club had received many enquiries, however, and parents who already had arrangements in place had indicated they were pleased the service was available and could be used if regular arrangements broke down. Nevertheless, the Club needed to regularly fill eight to 10 places for financial viability and was taking steps to increase utilisation. It was planning to open the service to outside users, although priority would be given to NHS employees should the Club become full. Such a step had proved successful in ensuring sustainability when the day nursery was first opened and until demand within the NHS had become established. Other ways to stimulate demand and to ensure cost-effectiveness and sustainability for the Club were under consideration, such as offering childcare for Christmas shopping days and a crèche. Users of the Club did not have to be working that day to use it.

Financial viability clearly depends on there being sufficient demand. As the national organisations pointed out, most childcare services rely on parental fees, and it is not cost-effective for group care to remain open if only a handful of parents need it. It is also difficult to sustain a service while demand is established. In an earlier survey of childcare providers, the time taken to fill vacancies and financial viability were two key obstacles which hindered the development of services (Callender, 2000). The consequence is that financial support is required either in the form of grants to providers or subsidies to parents. It was suggested by several of those whom we interviewed for our case studies that the government should provide tax credits, either to parents or directly to providers, which recognised the higher cost of childcare during unsocial working hours.

Many respondents saw sustainability as a real problem, particularly since 'pump-priming' grants were time-limited. One year's funding did not provide sufficient time for services to find alternative means of funding. For example, new childminding networks, which are eligible for government funding, have to become self-financing after the first year. As the manager of a Children's Information Service (CIS) put it: "We

are setting people up to offer specific services, raise standards and expect additional support and training, only to find that this is withdrawn if they are unsuccessful in finding alternative funding".

It took over six months to negotiate the contract for the childminding network with the Avon and Somerset Police Constabulary. Although funding is only for one year, it is hoped that the network will prove successful and secure further funding for a longer period. But it was generally considered that 'pump-priming' did not allow sufficient time for such negotiations, which often took much longer: "It takes a long time to get employers 'on board'. You have to raise awareness, often organise pilots to establish feasibility and make a business case, and attend meetings of the board and trustees" (National Childminding Association Development Worker).

Around a quarter of EYDCPs reported that lack of support from employers in their community was a barrier to developing services. One coordinator felt that small- and medium-sized businesses, which make up the majority of employers, were likely to need incentives to support childcare providers to offer these services. Whereas some national childcare organisations said that employers should be expected to meet some of the costs, others did not, or thought they would not do so.

Securing funding for new projects can be a complex process and both labour intensive and time consuming. There are many funding streams, and projects often have to apply to more than one. The Community Nanny Scheme provides a good example of these complexities. The EYDCP had funded the coordinator's post for one year during which time she had to secure funding for the project including her own post. It took nine months of her 12-month contract for her to do so. To cover the running costs of the project, applications were made to three funders. A positive response was received from the first funder in August, but the coordinator's salary was to be covered by a second funder who did not reach a decision until September. Not only did one funder give the project 50% less than had been asked for, which meant reducing the hours budgeted for community nannies from 60 to 30, but also the project was unsuccessful with one of the three bids. This left a shortfall of £30,000 on the overall budget. However, applications to funders often have to illustrate how the project will be funded in total and therefore include the other sources of money. The project has eventually received financial support to cover three years, but 18 months before this funding finishes the coordinator must start the process of finding alternative income once again.

It could be argued that such projects should not go ahead when future funding is too uncertain. Yet the need to develop childcare for lone parents (covering both standard and non-standard hours) had been identified in the EYDCP's local childcare audit, and the fact that the project was full and had a waiting list demonstrates that demand for such a service exists. Business plans drawn up as part of funding applications are required to consider how projects will manage financially once current funding ends. There is no guarantee that alternative funding, which is likely to mean parental fees or support from employers if charitable and government sources have been exhausted, will be forthcoming for projects such as the Community Nanny Scheme. But if the project had not gone ahead because of uncertainty about long-term viability, those families who currently use it would have been deprived of a much valued service.

To secure each year's funding, it is important for projects to achieve their set targets. In the example of the Community Nanny Scheme, funders want to see that the project is reaching as many families as possible and making a difference to those families. The project has to show how it will become sustainable, in their case by increasing their income through fees. However, the parents who the scheme has been set up to help are not earning enough (the true cost of a nanny in this scheme is £18 an hour, but the maximum a parent pays is £6 an hour, with fees set on a sliding scale). A further complication is that whereas one source of funding covers the total cost of childcare so that it can be offered free, the other requires a charge to be made. When families first make an enquiry, it is necessary to establish their financial circumstances to determine which 'pot' of money the childcare will come from. So, while there is one project, there are two administrative systems for funding.

Both the coordinator for this scheme and others we interviewed talked about the difficulties such situations created, especially the time involved in the monitoring and evaluation systems. Although monitoring is important, the time it takes can outweigh the time spent on project development. A plea was made for streamlining these systems to avoid duplication and the time needed to complete forms, submit reports, and so on.

Registration and inspection

Almost half of day nurseries and between a quarter and a third of other services perceived registration requirements for overnight care as a barrier. New childcare standards for overnight care came into effect in September 2001, when the Office for Standards in Education (OFSTED) took over the responsibility for the registration and inspection of early years and childcare services (DfES, 2001c). Previously, a provider's registration included overnight care automatically. The coordinator of the Children's Information Service (CIS) in one of the two areas sampled for the provider survey commented that the registration data supplied to them by OFSTED indicated fewer providers registered for overnight care than had previously been the case before the introduction of national standards and the involvement of OFSTED. This is only one CIS and the situation may not be repeated nationally. Nevertheless, inspectors need to think about the way in which they ask providers if they require registration for overnight care. If they are asked in a way that suggests they are unlikely to need it, as this coordinator suggested was sometimes happening, another barrier to developing services at atypical times is inadvertently set up.

The Community Nanny Scheme was registered in August 2001 before OFSTED assumed responsibility. From the project's inception, the coordinator had a close working relationship with the Registration and Inspection Unit in the local authority, which was seen as critical in establishing the service. The unit's support, together with the support from the EYDCP, was viewed as influential in securing funding for the project. Although the scheme awaits the transitional OFSTED inspection[1], the coordinator foresees problems since the scheme does not fit neatly into OFSTED's criteria for full day care nor the documentation in use. The Saturday Club has recently been registered, but had experienced some delay and difficulties because they, too, do not fit neatly into an existing childcare category but fall somewhere between a pre-school playgroup, crèche, nursery and out-of-school facility. Innovative services such as these do not have a network of established services to turn to for advice with such problems, and the delays and difficulties can become disheartening.

Both services also described the long delays in obtaining Criminal Records Bureau (CRB) checks for staff and the implications this had on their service. A community nanny had been waiting almost seven months for clearance and during this time was unable to work for the scheme. Such delays can postpone opening of a service and cause staff already recruited to look for another job. If a service has to wait too long before it can open, it may affect funding, since funders often require providers to start spending grants within 12 months. This problem applies to all childcare services and not only those offering childcare at atypical times.

The development of a sitter service (where registered childcare workers provide care in the child's home) had been delayed in one EYDCP because there was no clear guidance on the registration of home carers. Some of our respondents wanted a change in legislation with respect to registration of home-based childcare because currently there were inequities between, for example, nannies, foster carers and childminders. For example, nannies do not need to register with OFSTED unless they are caring for children from more than two families, whereas all childminders must register unless they are closely related to the child or are caring for a child for less than two hours a day.

Premises

Having suitable premises with the space and appropriate sleeping arrangements to

accommodate evening and overnight care is an important requirement. Settings that can provide space for children to have an afternoon nap may not be able to accommodate the needs of overnight care. Staff at the Children's Centre and Saturday Club had given careful thought to space. The extension at the Centre provided dedicated space for evening and weekend care. The childcare room has plenty of soft furnishings, dimmed lighting if required and a generally 'cosy' feel. National childcare organisations and more than a quarter of providers mentioned the problem of premises, pre-school playgroups in particular, although out-of-school services were also affected:

"Our preschool is run in the crypt of a church which is in use at other times."
(Pre-school playgroup)

"It is difficult to stay open too late in the evenings as this is a school, and rent would be too much." (After-school club)

The Pre-School Learning Alliance (PLA) told us how pre-school playgroups were finding it difficult to find suitable accommodation for all-day care. Because of these difficulties, the PLA felt it may be necessary for the government to help the voluntary sector with capital costs if they are to develop extended hours care.

Training and support

Few providers thought that different skills were needed to care for children during atypical hours: "nursery nurse training covers all aspects of childcare" (Children's Centre). Although all the community nannies are qualified nursery nurses, Kath (the nanny in our case study) was of the opinion that community nannies ideally needed to have some experience of working with parents too. Although the purpose of the scheme is to provide childcare for lone parents, many families have problems whether working or not, and nannies often find themselves providing family support as well as childcare. Less experienced nannies could find it difficult to talk to parents and advise them without undermining the parents' confidence.

Most childminders in the NHS Trust network were already active in childminder groups, and

---

[1] This refers to the first inspection by OFSTED for all providers registered at the time of transition of responsibility to OFSTED.

hence more likely to see childminding as a career. Length of time working as a childminder in the Avon and Somerset network varied from those who were new to childminding to those who had been childminding for some years. Our case study networks had not yet identified specific training needs associated with non-standard hours childcare, although information on issues such as bathing, bed-wetting and waking in the night might be required.

During our interviews for the case studies, the issue arose of the support that is available for childcare workers working atypical hours. Although childminders could access support during standard working hours, there was no support system in place should an emergency occur outside these hours. This would require support services, as well as childcare providers, to be available outside normal working hours. This was the case with the coordinator for the Community Nanny Scheme, who was on call while nannies were working. But this meant that, in addition to her standard 36 hours a week, she was on call for another 25 hours.

A quarter of EYDCPs thought that lack of government support and guidance was a barrier to service development, while a quarter thought that government support had helped in developing services. Some national childcare organisations felt that there should be better links between services to help meet the needs of parents working atypical hours, and that EYDCPs could facilitate this. Another suggested that government could give encouragement to Neighbourhood Nurseries and Early Excellence Centres to build atypical hours care into their plans. Schools were also seen as having a possible role by acting as a hub for access to services, which covered both standard and non-standard hours.

Children's welfare

Many of our respondents, including providers, the organisations representing them and EYDCPs, questioned the appropriateness of formal childcare to cover atypical working hours, particularly in the early morning, late evening and overnight. Weekend and extended hours care (between 7am and 7pm) seemed to raise less concern. Worries were expressed about the

quality of family life and whether atypical hours childcare was good for children: "Children like to be in their own home and sleep in their own bed" (childminder). The belief that children needed to be with their families at these times was mentioned by over half of day nurseries and over a third of other services in our survey (Table 3.3).

"I strongly believe that children should be at home during the evenings and weekends and certainly overnight – otherwise I don't really see why people bother to have them." (Day nursery)

'I believe the longer hours of childcare offered, the longer parents will want. Children, particularly under fives, should be at home for breakfast and evening meal with their families, even a relative." (Day nursery)

Some respondents said that careful consideration should be given to children's needs as well as to meeting parents' needs. This necessitated looking at where services should be based, especially since atypical hours often involve long shifts, such as four 12-hour shifts a week, which is not the same as five standard days. Concern was expressed about the number of hours a child might be in childcare: "since the opening of the Saturday Club some children are attending six full days a week". The experience at the Children's Centre was that different children seemed to be using the evening and weekend service to the daytime service, and staff were not aware of children coming for six or seven days a week. They had adopted a policy that no child could attend more than 10 hours in any 24-hour period. There is little research evidence to show how children might be differentially affected by childcare depending on the hours they attend, although quality rather than quantity appears to be the most important factor (Mooney and Munton, 1997).

The case studies do show how services can try to take account of children's potentially different needs during atypical times. In the group-based provision, one of the most significant differences was the number of children: far fewer attend in the evening and at weekends. The time and number of children influence activities. In the evenings, staff described emphasising care and comfort more than education and organised

27

group activities. There was greater flexibility in routines and children had more choice, for example to watch television. At the Children's Centre, children under five were put in their nightwear if parents requested it, although there were no facilities for bathing.

The study by La Valle et al (2002) shows how important weekends are to parents as a time for being involved in their children's activities and being together as a family. The weekends are seen as being different by the group-based services in terms of the activities provided. More attention is given to creative and fun-filled activities geared to a mixed age range. Homework is not encouraged at the Saturday Club unless a child wants to bring it to do at the Club. There they have a room where children can 'hang out' and spend time together without close adult supervision. Getting it right for children also affects viability: "It is important to have activities that children want to do so that they will continue to attend the Club and publicise it to their friends" (NHS childcare coordinator). When more children are enrolled, a children's committee is planned so that children themselves can have a say in what they want and influence decisions.

Our case study childminder, Ann, also drew a distinction between weekday and weekend care, but in a rather different way. Whereas she organised specific activities and outings for children during the week, at the weekends it was very much a case of fitting in with her family's routines and activities. Her husband was registered as her assistant and was actively involved in childcare at the weekends.

Although ensuring continuity of care was not seen as a major barrier to developing atypical hours childcare by survey respondents, some of the provider organisations suggested that continuity could be more difficult to achieve when care was needed at these times. This was potentially an issue at the Children's Centre, where nursery nurses from the 'bank' staffed the evening and weekend service. The Centre made every effort to ensure that children with a regular booking had the same staff, but they might not be with the same children. Parents' changing shift patterns meant there was little continuity in the group of children from one week to the next.

Which services are most suitable for providing childcare at atypical times?

Childminders were generally seen as the most appropriate form of provision by EYDCP coordinators and also by some of the national childcare organisations. This was because the costs for centre-based providers are prohibitive and therefore it is difficult to make such provision financially viable; because parents cannot afford the premium rates required to make it cost-effective; and because services anticipated difficulties in recruiting staff willing to work at atypical times. Childminders were also perceived as offering continuity and "a 'homelike' environment, which may be more important for non-standard hours care, particularly overnight care" (EYDCP). However, those advocating childminders as the best providers of non-standard hours care also recognised that there were real issues to address, such as the childminders' own work–life balance and the danger of working long hours, and how to accommodate childcare that covered standard and non-standard hours in terms of ratios and income. While home-based childcare, such as childminders, was often viewed as the most appropriate provision for atypical hours, there was concern about an over-reliance on this group of providers: "Pressure seems to be on childminders to extend their hours. [They are] expected to bend and stretch their service to offer greater flexibility" (CIS manager).

Others pointed to the diverse childcare needs of parents and the fact that a 'one size fits all' approach is unlikely to work. They highlighted the need for universal, integrated services, including a mix of home-based and centre-based care so that parents could 'mix and match' to suit their needs. One suggested way forward was to have centres with homecarers attached, with partnerships taking a stronger role in coordinating and linking services to parents' needs. Another suggestion was for a 24-hour centre-based service operating on a rolling rota, and large enough to support a drop-in crèche and out-of-school provision. There are examples of centres operating a 24-hour day, seven-day week in the US (US DLWB, 1995).

Advice from those who have developed services covering atypical hours

We asked those we interviewed for the case studies what advice they would give to those wanting to develop services to cover atypical working hours. All made the point that it takes a long time to develop services and it cannot be achieved 'overnight'. *"Don't give up!"* was the advice from the NHS childcare coordinator. Respondents talked about needing a long-term vision and the need to think imaginatively in resolving difficulties. Proper costings were also essential and consideration should be given to issues of sustainability. Undertaking as much research as possible, especially talking to parents, providers and agencies before setting up, was also important.

Summary

Services are only just starting to be developed to meet the needs of parents working at atypical times, and there is little experience to draw on yet. A few innovative schemes have been set up, including childminding networks, sitter services such as the community nanny scheme, and centre-based weekend care. Not all are fully operational yet, and a recurring theme in our study was that developing such services takes considerable time.

Although most EYDCPs believe that there is a need to develop childcare at atypical times, less than a third have tried to encourage providers to do so. Childminders were generally seen as the most appropriate type of provision to develop atypical hours care because of their home base. There was some concern, however, about an over-reliance of the strategy on childminders to fill this gap in services, because this might affect their well-being, their own families and the children they cared for.

The most common barrier to service development has been the reluctance of childcare workers to work non-standard hours, primarily because of the impact on their own family, followed by financial considerations such as sustainability and costs, especially when parental demand appears to be low. Another concern was that it is not in children's best interest to be cared for at such times by anyone other than a family member. Yet, this study also shows that some childcare workers are willing or able to work at atypical times and that developing new services in this area is possible. However, there are a number of barriers or constraints that need to be overcome, which include: creating sufficient demand, funding and sustainability; combining non-standard and standard hours childcare, registration and inspection requirements; premises; and support for providers.

4

Conclusion

Under the National Childcare Strategy there has been a significant expansion of early years education and childcare services. Nevertheless, there is still some way to go to achieve access to good quality, affordable childcare for every parent, even during standard working hours. Providing affordable childcare at atypical times presents an additional challenge. Yet such care is likely to become increasingly necessary as the growth of a '24-hour society' is creating new working patterns, while at the same time traditional sources of childcare, such as grandparents, are becoming increasingly unavailable. In this final chapter, we review the barriers to developing services for atypical hours identified in our study, and consider their policy implications.

Recruiting the workforce

As we have shown, a key stumbling block to making childcare more widely available at non-standard times is the reluctance expressed by many existing childcare providers to working atypical hours (although it should be noted that many childminders are already offering a flexible service with an early start). Eighty per cent of childcare providers in our survey said they were unwilling to work overnight or at weekends, and the majority of group day care services cited the difficulty of finding staff to work atypical hours as a barrier to developing this provision. Nevertheless, our case studies demonstrate that the development of existing or new services has been possible. There are likely to be local factors affecting willingness to work atypical hours, such as a high number of vacancies in childcare services creating the need to attract new customers, or a local labour market which creates a significant demand for atypical hours care.

Targeting childcare workers at different periods in the life course

Individual factors, such as the provider's own family circumstances, are also likely to have an impact. In developing services to accommodate work at atypical times, the work–life balance of childcare providers themselves needs to be considered. Many have young children of their own. It would be ironic if, by encouraging them to extend their hours of work to provide childcare for parents working atypical hours, their own work–life balance was thereby sacrificed. Those without childcare responsibilities themselves may be more willing to work at atypical times, suggesting that targeting people at different stages in their life course may be appropriate. Alternatively, rather than expecting existing providers to extend their service, another approach would be to develop new forms of childcare to cover atypical hours.

New types of service

Some of the provision covering non-standard hours that we have described in this report has been developed from existing services, as in the case of the Abacus Children's Centre in London and the Saturday Club in Birmingham. But new types of service, such as the Community Nanny Scheme, might be particularly suited to care for children at atypical times. Childminding networks could also offer a promising way forward. Groups of childminders working together, providing care in their own home but able to provide 'cover' for colleagues at times when they are unable to offer a service, could allow childminders to provide atypical hours care without requiring individual providers to work even longer hours than they already do. The downside is a potential reduction in continuity of care for children, but such arrangements appear to work in countries such as Sweden, where groups of childminders meet regularly, together with the children they care for, and so children are familiar with other potential caregivers (Karllson, 2003). Childminding networks as they are developing in the UK offer access to quality assurance mechanisms, support, additional training and business opportunities, and could encourage the development of good quality childcare provision that would meet the needs of parents working atypical hours.

Regulating new services

Developing such new services does, however, pose challenges to current registration and inspection procedures. So far, little thought seems to have been given to issues such as the appropriate adult:child ratios for overnight care, or the standards that need to be met if a community nanny is providing care in a child's own home. If childcare is needed at varying and unpredictable times, most services will also need to combine this with caring for children during standard working hours, in order to remain economically viable. Yet this is likely to make it difficult to maintain consistent adult:child ratios. Such new services are only now emerging, so it is not surprising that the issues they raise have yet to be addressed, but a review of OFSTED procedures for registering and inspecting services that deviate from traditional models may be necessary in the near future.

Working conditions

A more fundamental issue, which is likely to affect the willingness of childcare providers to work at atypical times, is the poor pay and low status attached to childcare work generally. Recruiting and retaining more childcare workers, whether this is to provide atypical or standard hours care, is giving the government some cause for concern. Urgent attention needs to be given to the working conditions and pay of this sector of the workforce if the situation is to improve (Cameron et al, 2001; Mooney et al, 2001).

Funding and sustainability

One of the dilemmas of improving the pay of childcare workers is that this increases the cost of care to parents. Although a third of all providers said that the ability to charge a higher fee would encourage them to offer childcare at atypical times, almost the same proportion recognised that parents could not afford to pay more. Furthermore, the parents most likely to need childcare at these times are often least likely to be in a position to pay, as the Community Nanny Scheme in Bradford illustrates. It is doubtful whether asking parents to pay more for atypical hours childcare is the answer to service development and financial viability, unless fees can be sufficiently subsidised, for example through tax credits or employer support.

Tax credits

Parents on low incomes have been eligible for help with childcare costs through the Childcare Tax Credit, part of the Working Families' Tax Credit. But this has not reached many families: figures released in 2002 showed that only 2.3% of all families in England with children up to the age of 16 were receiving the benefit (Ward, 2002). A new system introduced in April 2003 replaced these with Child Tax Credit and Working Tax Credit. Eligibility for the childcare element of this new system of tax credits will be extended to those who use approved childcare in their own homes. The government argues that this will "benefit, in particular, parents of disabled children and those who work outside conventional hours" (HM Treasury and DTI, 2003, foreword). So far, approved home-based childcare only covers registered childminders working in the child's home, so parents using the community nanny scheme would not be eligible for the tax credit as the nannies are not registered childminders. However, consideration is being given to how those who are not already childminders can be included in the scheme. It remains to be seen how these changes in the tax credit system will benefit parents and the development of services.

Business planning and short-term funding

Sustainability is a real issue for childcare services, and many out-of-school clubs and newly-developed services face a real struggle to keep going. One point of view would be that this reflects a lack of business planning, since if the market had been properly researched and the business plan indicated a problem with financial viability in the future, projects should not have started. But if this were applied, many services which in the long-term prove successful would never get 'off the ground'. It is true that many childcare providers do not have a business management background – their work is childcare not running a business, although this is what many are required to do. With this is mind, many EYDCPs now have an adviser who provides help with business plans and financial issues and the government has recently announced new funding to provide business training and support for up to 100,000 businesses within the childcare sector (Evans, 2003). However, services are likely to spend a high proportion of their time on seeking funding, and on monitoring and evaluating their work to satisfy funding requirements. There is a tension between the justifiable need to demonstrate what works, and the often time-consuming process of developing and nurturing a new service. Streamlining these procedures and the different funding streams that services can access would be another way of encouraging and supporting service development. This was acknowledged in the government's interdepartmental review of childcare at the end of 2002, which concluded that there are too many uncoordinated programmes and that delivery mechanisms need to be reformed (DFES et al, 2002).

However, the problem is not simply that providers fail to do their business homework. It is also that they are providing a service within a system that depends on market forces, supplemented by short-term 'pump priming' sources of funding. Most childminding networks, for example, receive funding for only one year before having to become self-financing. This provides little time to establish and develop the service as well as find alternative sources of funding.

Employer support

Support from employers could improve sustainability. However, despite the example of the NHS, few employers have introduced employment strategies recognising the specific needs of mothers with young children. In a recent survey of 2,000 human resources managers, only 8% said their organisations offered any financial assistance to employees for childcare costs (Taylor, 2002). The same survey found that just 3% provided any childcare facilities, either on site or elsewhere, and 12% provided information to their employees on childcare in their locality. The report concluded that "companies do not appear to believe they are under any special obligation to assist women employees with their child care arrangements" (Taylor, 2002, p 16).

This presents a challenge to EYDCPs, which have been set targets to increase the amount of support that employers provide. Although the costs of supporting childcare are tax deductible for employers, these findings suggest that further incentives may be needed to encourage employers to contribute. The government is considering how the tax and National Insurance contributions exemptions on employer-supported childcare could be improved, "including how they could offer a better incentive to employers to support childcare provision" (HM Treasury and DTI, 2003, p 40). An alternative would be a compulsory levy on employers in general to fund childcare costs, as is the case in France and Belgium (Candappa et al, 2003: forthcoming).

Parental demand for services covering atypical hours

Sustaining a childcare service once it is set up is important, but the other side of the coin is establishing whether there is a demand from parents for the service in the first place. The growth of a '24-hour society' is requiring increasing numbers of people, including those with children, to work outside the hours that formal childcare services have traditionally operated. It would be expected that this would create a demand for services to extend their hours, or for new services to be developed which can meet parents' need for atypical hours care. Our study did indeed show some unmet demand. One in five childcare providers reported that they had at some time been asked by parents to provide care between 6pm and 8pm, but had been unable or unwilling to do so. Around one in eight had been unable to meet a parent's request for care before 8am, at times that varied from week to week, overnight or at the weekend.

However, few EYDCPs perceived a significant demand for such care, and representatives of national childcare organisations generally thought that the demand for atypical hours care was mostly limited to services that extended an hour or so at each end of the day. In addition, those childcare services that were developing non-standard hours care often reported difficulty in sustaining provision because of low take-up.

Difficulties in establishing demand

One conclusion could be that although there is some demand for atypical hours childcare, the demand is not sufficient to justify service development. However, the information upon which demand is assessed is not as robust as we would like. Providers may not perceive a demand because they have received few requests for the service. But parents who believe a service to be unavailable may not ask for it. Nor do we really know what parents would choose if affordable, high quality formal services were available. The traditional patchwork of fragmented services has often been inadequate to meet the childcare needs of families. Parents may use informal care in these circumstances for a variety of reasons, for example to eliminate the costs of formal childcare (LaValle et al, 2002) or to avoid the complexity of trying to coordinate different childcare arrangements (Skinner, 2003). Some parents in two-parent families manage their childcare needs by 'shift parenting', where one parent takes over as the other leaves for work. But this can have negative consequences for family life, and leave the adults with little time to spend together (La Valle et al, 2002). It is also not an option for lone parents.

Many parents choose to use partners/ex-partners, other relatives and friends because this is their preference. Grandparents are considered an ideal childcare option by around two thirds of working mothers, and friends and neighbours ideal by around a half (Woodland et al, 2002).

But not all parents have access to this form of care, or, if they do, may lose it if one parent's career requires job relocation (Green and Canny, 2003). Demographic and employment trends also mean that such informal sources of childcare are likely to be in increasingly short supply in the future, as more women in their fifties and sixties remain in paid employment and/or have other caring responsibilities such as for elderly parents (Mooney and Statham, 2002).

Parents' decisions and choices about childcare are often complex and take account of several factors, such as availability and affordability (Moss et al, 1998). Choosing childcare is an emotional as well as a practical decision, and this increases the difficulty of judging demand. Parents may say they would like alternative services, such as a nursery or childminder offering non-standard hours, but this does not always mean that they would use it. This also applies to childcare during standard hours. Changing childcare is not like changing a car or trying out different product brands. Children become attached to their carer, and it is known that close adult–child attachments and continuity of care are important for children's development (Mooney and Munton, 1997). Given these circumstances, parents do not readily move their children to another childcare arrangement just because a new service has become available. However, they may well use the service if their current arrangement broke down, and new parents may also use it. New services, whether covering standard or non-standard hours, take time to establish and for demand to build. It is the same when a new school opens – the school is not full from day one, but may take three or four years to reach this stage. This does not suggest that the school was not needed.

Children's needs

One of the factors that influence the use of childcare is parents' – and society's – beliefs about what is good for children. There is a common perception that children are better off at home with their parent(s), or at least with family and friends, outside of standard working hours. While the use of childcare during 'normal' working hours is now largely accepted as having benefits for children's learning and socialisation, as well as enabling their parents to work, the use of formal care services during non-standard times can cause more of a problem. Care outside the family at these times was still regarded with ambivalence and sometimes outright hostility by many of the childcare providers in our survey. The findings from different parts of our study suggest that the degree to which atypical hours care is seen as acceptable depends on a combination of when it is needed and how it is provided. Generally, informal care by relatives or family (broadly defined) is seen as most acceptable, while home-based formal childcare, such as childminding, is seen as more acceptable than centre-based care because the latter is more institutional. But acceptability also depends on the time the care is provided. Leaving a child in a 'Saturday club' for half a day may be viewed more favourably than leaving the same child with a home-based care service in the late evening or overnight. Some of the times when childcare may need to be provided seemed in our study to be especially problematic, notably late evenings and overnight. The view was also expressed that weekends were somehow sacrosanct and children needed to be with their families at this time.

Are these views supported by research? There is little evidence to show whether or not children are adversely affected by being in formal childcare services at atypical times. Other studies have shown how many parents regard evening meals as an important time, which provide an opportunity for them to spend some 'quality' time together as a family (La Valle et al, 2002). Yet, based on little evidence, assumptions are made that if children do not share most evening meals together or every weekend, this will be detrimental. There is little evidence on this topic, and it would be useful to obtain more information in this area and to engage in a broader debate about children's place in society, and about ways of achieving a balance between children's and parents' needs and the requirements of paid work.

Family-friendly workplaces

Many parents dislike working non-standard hours, especially when this is not through choice, because of its effect on family life such as reducing their involvement in their children's activities or giving them less time to spend together as a couple (La Valle et al, 2002). Alongside developing atypical hours childcare services, it is important to consider how employment policies and working hours could be made more 'family friendly', so that parents have less need for care at such times in the first place. It can be very difficult to arrange childcare if shifts rotate over a three- or four-week period, if weekend work is required at short notice, or if parents regularly need to work late hours or overnight. Yet, apart from part-time employment, only a small proportion of workplaces provide flexible working time arrangements (Hogarth et al, 2001). This is despite the fact that there is some evidence (Dex and Smith, 2002; Gray, 2002) that family-friendly work practices are associated with improved business performance in private sector firms.

A recent government report on balancing work and family life highlights the government's commitment "to working with business to encourage the adoption of best practice and offer flexible working opportunities throughout the workforce" (HM Treasury and DTI, 2003, p 37).

The Work–Life Balance Campaign, launched in 2000, aims to encourage employers to implement policies and practices which promote flexible working. The campaign includes guides and publications for businesses, funding to provide advice to employers, and funding for projects which improve employees' work–life balance. Since April 2003, parents of young children also have a right to request flexible working and have this request seriously considered by their employer. The development of childcare services to cover non-standard working hours does not eliminate the need to consider critically how working conditions, including the 'long hours' culture that is gaining an increased foothold in the UK, could be adapted to better meet the needs of parents and children.

Summary of policy implications

In summary, the main policy issues arising from our study, with the groups to which they are addressed in brackets, are:

- developing new types of service, for example community nanny/sitter schemes (EYDCPs, employers, childcare providers);

- reviewing registration requirements for overnight and home-based care (OFSTED);
- recruiting childcare workers at different stages of the life course, for example those without young children of their own (EYDCPs, childcare services);
- improving the pay and status of childcare work (government, national childcare organisations, trades unions);
- creating partnerships and networks between childcare providers, including links between home-based and centre-based services (government, EYDCPs, national childcare organisations);
- support from employers for childcare to cover atypical hours (employers, trades unions);
- developing family-friendly working practices (government, employers, trades unions);
- streamlining funding and monitoring processes (government, EYDCPs, other funding bodies);
- extending 'pump-priming' funding and support for capital costs (government, EYDCPs, other funding bodies, employers);
- system of tax credits or other subsidies to make atypical hours childcare affordable for all parents who need it (government, employers);
- inclusion of atypical hours childcare in plans for the Neighbourhood Nurseries Initiative and Early Excellence Centres (government, EYDCPs);
- debate and further research about what is best for children when parents are working at atypical times (government, researchers, society in general).

It is clear that significant development of childcare outside standard working hours is unlikely to be achieved, at least at the current stage of development, without government or employer support. Even with increased parental demand, such services will find it difficult to achieve financial viability, at least in the short term. Our case studies illustrated the importance of funding for an infrastructure to support the development of atypical hours care, such as a coordinator or scheme organiser who can match families with providers offering childcare at the times that they need.

Ideally, atypical hours care needs to be seen as one part of a coherent range of services that address the varying needs of children and families – not only childcare so that parents can work, but also education and stimulation for children, advice and support for parents, and the development of strong local communities. Current policy developments to integrate children's services, for example through the Neighbourhood Nurseries Initiative, Sure Start programme and proposed Children's Centres, show how this can be done. If we view childcare at atypical times merely as something to be bolted onto existing services, requiring providers to work even longer hours than many already do, we miss the opportunity of thinking how services could be brought together to meet the needs of all those involved, not least the children.

References

Bell, I. (2000) 'Employment rates 1959-1999', *Labour Market Trends*, January, pp 35-9.

Bell, A. and La Valle, I. (2003) *Combining self-employment and family life*, Bristol/York: The Policy Press/Joseph Rowntree Foundation.

Brannen, J., Moss, P., Owen, C. and Wale, C. (1997) *Mothers, fathers and employment: Parents and the labour market in Britain 1984-1994*, DfEE Research Report No 10, London: DfEE.

Callender, C. (2000) *The barriers to childcare provision*, DfEE Research Report RR231, London: DfEE.

Cameron, C., Mooney, A., Owen, C. and Moss, P. (2001) *Childcare students and nursery workers: Follow up survey and in-depth interviews*, DfES Research Report RR322, London: DfES.

Candappa, M., Moss, P., Cameron, C., McQuail, S., Mooney, A. and Petrie, P. (2003: forthcoming) *Early years and childcare international evidence project: Funding and sustainability*, London: DfES.

Daycare Trust (2000) *No more nine to five: Childcare in a changing world*, London: Daycare Trust.

Daycare Trust (2001) *NHS childcare toolkit*, London: Daycare Trust and Department of Health.

Daycare Trust (2002) *NHS childcare toolkit II: Beyond workplace nurseries*, London: Daycare Trust and Department of Health.

Dex, S. and Smith, C. (2002) *The nature and pattern of family-friendly employment policies in Britain*, Bristol/York: The Policy Press/Joseph Rowntree Foundation.

DfEE (Department for Education and Employment) (1998) *The National Childcare Strategy*, London: DfEE.

DfEE (2001) *Early years development and childcare partnership planning guidance 2001-2002*, London: DfEE.

DfEE (2000) *Children's day care facilities at 31 March 2000: England*, London: DfEE.

DfES (Department for Education and Skills) (2001a) *Childcare and atypical work*, Early Years Development and Childcare Partnerships Report 42, London: DfES.

DfES (2001b) *Children's day care facilities at 31 March 2001, England*, Statistical Bulletin 8/01, London: DfES.

DfES (2001c) *National standards for day care and childminding*, London: DfES.

Department for Education and Skills/Department for Work and Pensions/HM Treasury/Women and Equality Unit (2002) *Delivering for children and families: Inter-departmental childcare review*, London: Strategy Unit.

European Union (1998) *The Working Time Regulations: Statutory Instrument 1998 No 1833*, London: The Stationery Office.

Evans, M. (2003) *Business training: Missing links*, Nursery World 17 April available at www.nursery-world.co.uk

Gray, H. (2002) *Family-friendly working: What a performance! An analysis of the relationship between the availability of family-friendly policies and establishment performance*, London: Centre for Economic Performance.

Green, A. and Canny, A. (2003) *Geographical mobility: Employee relocation and its family impacts*, Bristol/York: The Policy Press/Joseph Rowntree Foundation.

HM Treasury and DTI (Department of Trade and Industry) (2003) *Balancing work and family life: Enhancing choice and support for parents*, Norwich: The Stationery Office.

Hogarth, T., Hasluck, C. and Pierre, G. (2001) *Work–life balance 2000: Results from the Baseline Study*, DfEE Research Report No 249, London: DfEE.

Karllson, M. (2003) 'The everyday life of children in family day care as seen by their carers', in A. Mooney and J. Statham (eds) *Family day care: International perspectives on policy, practice and quality*, London: Jessica Kingsley Publishers, pp 148-62.

Kelleher, C. (2000) 'Childcare for all: looking back ... looking forward', *Childcare Now*, Issue 12, pp 1 and 4.

La Valle, I., Arthur, S., Millward, C., Scott, J. with Clayden, M. (2002) *Happy families? Atypical work and its influence on family life*, Bristol/York: The Policy Press/Joseph Rowntree Foundation.

Mooney, A. and Munton, A.G. (1997) *Research and policy in early childhood services: Time for a new agenda*, London: Institute of Education, University of London.

Mooney, A. and Statham, J. with Simon, A. (2002) *The pivot generation: Informal care and work after fifty*, Bristol/York: The Policy Press/Joseph Rowntree Foundation.

Mooney, A., Knight, A., Moss, P. and Owen, C. (2001) *Who cares? Childminding in the 1990s*, Bristol/York: The Policy Press/Joseph Rowntree Foundation.

Moss, P., Mooney, A., Munton, A.G. and Statham, J. (1998) *Local assessments of childcare need and provision*, London: DfEE.

Moss, P., Owen, C., Statham, J., Bull, J., Cameron, C. and Candappa, M. (1995) *Survey of daycare providers in England and Wales*, London: Thomas Coram Research Unit.

NHS (National Health Service) (2000) *The NHS Plan: A plan for investment, a plan for reform*. London: The Stationery Office.

Skinner, C. (2003) *Running around in circles: Coordinating childcare, education and work*, Bristol/York: The Policy Press/Joseph Rowntree Foundation.

Statham, J., Holtermann, S. and Stone, M. (1996) *Childcare in Wales: The 1996 audit*, Cardiff: Children in Wales.

Strategy Unit (2002) *Delivering for children and families: Inter-departmental childcare review*, London: DfES, Department for Work and Pensions, HM Treasury, Women and Equality Unit, Strategy Unit.

Taylor, R. (2002) *Managing workplace change*, ESRC Future of Work Programme Seminar Series, Swindon: Economic and Social Research Council.

TUC (Trades Union Congress) (2002) *About time: A new agenda for shaping working life*. London: TUC.

Tweed, J. (2002) Pre-schools stuck in limited facilities, *Nursery World*, 21 November, pp 4-5.

Twomey, B. (2001) 'Women in the labour market: results from the spring 2000 LFS', *Labour Market Trends*, February, pp 93-106.

US DLWB (Department of Labor and Women's Bureau) (1995) 'Care around the clock: developing child care resources before nine and after five', at http://nccic.org/pubs/carecloc.html.

Ward, L. (2002) 'Childcare policy fails to help poor', *The Guardian*, 19 December.

Woodland, S., Miller, M. and Tipping, S. (2002) *Repeat study of parents' demand for childcare*, Research Report 348, London: DfES.